By the same author

365 Steps to Self Confidence
365 Ways to be your own Life Coach
365 Steps to Practical Spirituality

201
THINGS ABOUT CHRISTIANITY YOU PROBABLY DON'T KNOW

(But Ought To)

DAVID LAWRENCE PRESTON

BALBOA.
PRESS
A DIVISION OF HAY HOUSE

New Revised Standard Version Bible: Anglicised Edition, copyright © 1989, 1995
the Division of Christian Education of the National Council of the Churches of
Christ in the United States of America. Used by permission. All rights reserved.

Balboa Press books may be ordered through booksellers or by contacting:

Balboa Press
A Division of Hay House
1663 Liberty Drive
Bloomington, IN 47403
www.balboapress.com
1 (877) 407-4847

Because of the dynamic nature of the Internet, any web addresses or
links contained in this book may have changed since publication and
may no longer be valid. The views expressed in this work are solely those
of the author and do not necessarily reflect the views of the publisher,
and the publisher hereby disclaims any responsibility for them.

The author of this book does not dispense medical advice or prescribe the use
of any technique as a form of treatment for physical, emotional, or medical
problems without the advice of a physician, either directly or indirectly. The
intent of the author is only to offer information of a general nature to help
you in your quest for emotional and spiritual well-being. In the event you use
any of the information in this book for yourself, which is your constitutional
right, the author and the publisher assume no responsibility for your actions.

Any people depicted in stock imagery provided by Thinkstock are models,
and such images are being used for illustrative purposes only.
Certain stock imagery © Thinkstock.

Print information available on the last page.

ISBN: 978-1-5043-3697-0 (sc)
ISBN: 978-1-5043-3699-4 (hc)
ISBN: 978-1-5043-3698-7 (e)

Library of Congress Control Number: 2015911576

Balboa Press rev. date: 07/28/2015

DEDICATION

This book is dedicated in the spirit of Truth to
all my spiritual teachers, and to the memory of
Yeshua bar Yehosef, the greatest of them all.

CONTENTS

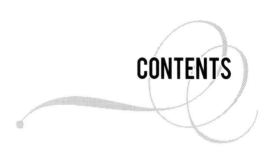

PREFACE

WHY DOES IT MATTER?

Christianity is the dominant faith in Europe, North America, Africa, South America, Australasia and large swathes of the East. Approximately a third of the world's population live in countries which consider themselves to be predominantly Christian. If you live in any of these countries, Christianity impacts on all areas of your life even if you are not a Christian. That's why it is important to understand where Christians are coming from.

In the country of my birth, the United Kingdom, Christianity is actively followed by a tiny fraction of the population, about one in twenty depending on how you define 'actively'. Only about one in fifty (2%) attend services regularly, and it is almost obsolete in the inner cities, but Christian thinking is woven into every strand of our national life. It has political, cultural, legal and social influence far beyond its numbers. Every street belongs to a parish, and many parishes elect a 'Parish Council' which plays an important part in the life of the area. Every town and village has a church, although few attract enough people to Sunday services to make up a cricket team. Some householders are even required to pay 'Chancel Tax' in the event their parish church needs repairs, even if they have never set foot in the church.

The Church of England is the established church, an integral part of the country's system of government even though it is not subject to the rigours of democratic control[1]. The monarch (hereditary and unelected) is its Supreme Governor; its archbishops are appointed by the monarch. Its senior bishops (appointed and unelected) have the right to sit in the Upper Chamber of Parliament, the House of Lords (whose members are unelected). The electorate don't have any say over who is chosen, that's just the way it is, and no government of any political party has ever tried to change it.

Ironically, Roman Catholics, who account for the largest proportion of active Christians in the UK, are barred from holding certain offices of state or marrying into the Royal Family. One recent Prime Minister, Tony Blair, didn't admit to Catholic sympathies until after leaving office for fear of jeopardising his electoral prospects, but nevertheless played his part in recommending bishops and archbishops for the Church of England. He was subsequently received officially into the Catholic Church.

Christian ideas are guaranteed a special airing in the media, since our revered national broadcaster, the BBC, and our leading commercial broadcaster are charged by law with ensuring that they deliver a specified minimum quantity of Christian content. There's a 'Prayer for the Day', 'Daily Worship' and a 'Thought for the Day' on the radio every morning, mostly of a Christian nature, and several hours of Christian programming on TV every Sunday, such as the 'Sunday Service' and 'Songs of Praise'.

Church dignitaries are invariably wheeled out on important national and military occasions. They're there at times of crisis,

---

[1] The Church of Scotland does not enjoy this status, nor do any of the churches in Wales and Northern Ireland which also make up the United Kingdom.

celebration and commemoration, often with members of the Royal Family and government conspicuous in the congregation alongside celebrities of one sort or another. When the bodies are brought back from foreign wars, Christian clergy lead the official mourning.

Church leaders also have easy access to the media. They can get their opinions on issues of social policy, economics, medicine, science, international affairs and so on across much more easily than other members of the public. Sometimes they even insist they have the right to override the law of the land, for instance over the implementation of equality and diversity legislation on gay marriage and adoption, although this doesn't usually wash in parliamentary circles these days.

The Christian religion also has a firm grip on the country's educational system. State schools are required to have a daily act of worship, predominantly Christian. In addition, a significant proportion of schools obtain a proportion of their funding from the Church of England or Catholic Church in exchange for a seat or two on the Governing Body, which bring influence over recruitment and the curriculum. In recent years the British government has encouraged other religions to have their schools too.

From time to time someone suggests that the Church of England should lose its preferential status since so few people attend church regularly and there are more Roman Catholics and Muslims in the UK than Anglicans. The result is howls of anguish from the establishment, as if the moral welfare of the nation would be irreparably damaged if the bishops were excluded from the corridors of power. Hence the UK government continues to hang on to discriminatory blasphemy laws which protect only one religion – Christianity. Obviously the powers that be feel that religion is above criticism and they need the full force of the law to protect them.

So there's no getting round it, not even for people who are not religious: if you live in a Western country, the Christian religion, its institutions and representatives play a huge role in governing you whether you like it or not and you have no say in this. In other countries, such as the United States, the church has no official status but many politicians owe their election to its support and few dare declare themselves non-Christian. (One exception was 2012 presidential candidate Mitt Romney, a Mormon, who was soundly beaten.) So if only for the sake of democracy we should all be concerned to know what Christians believe, where they claim their legitimacy and why their ideas and practices deserve such prominence. Then, if you wish, you can make your voice heard from an informed stance. That's why I wrote this book.

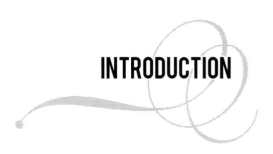

INTRODUCTION

1. Until the early 19th Century few people in the Christian world questioned the Bible's accuracy

The Christian religion is grounded in the Bible, which for a millennium and a half was considered sacrosanct. Until the early 19th Century few people in the Christian world dared to question the accuracy of the Bible. Only when the biblical texts began to be studied seriously in the early 1800s and cross referenced with other sources did a better understanding begin to emerge. As result, most Christians at that time had a very unrealistic view of Christian history and their religion, and now, two hundred years later, most still do:

- They don't know how their religion was founded, who wrote - or did not write – their sacred scripture, the New Testament scripts, when, or in what order.
- They've never compared the gospels and wondered why they differ so much both in content and detail.
- They have no idea how the religion developed over subsequent centuries.
- They can't even tell you the real name of their saviour, the language he spoke, or the language in which the New Testament was originally written.

But unless we understand how the New Testament came into being and how it ties in with the historical and archaeological records from that time, we will never understand Yeshua² and the religion that functions in his name.

My interest was triggered when a friend lent me a book called 'Joshua'. Written by a retired Catholic priest, Father Joseph Girzone, it tells the story of Yeshua's return to Earth as a humble carpenter in modern-day America. It's a heartening tale of a compassionate man who engages the local townsfolk with his warmth, wisdom and generosity. I won't spoil it by telling you what happens, except that he ends up being sent to Rome and thrown out of the Catholic Church for subverting their religion!

So impressed was I by this simple, down-to-earth tale that I started to explore the Christian scriptures. I read the New Testament cover to cover and attended Bible classes. I studied the Hebrew Scriptures (better known, misleadingly, as the 'Old Testament'). I rediscovered teachings about love, compassion, forgiveness and sharing that took me back to my childhood experiences as a regular attender in church and Sunday School. I put them into practice as best I could and found, somewhat to my surprise, that they made my life better. I went on to give talks on biblical wisdom and spirituality to many audiences. By then I had digested hundreds of books on personal development and practical psychology and found most of the gospel teachings compatible with the best of them. I even started referring to myself as a follower of Yeshua, which, ironically, brought me into conflict with some Christians!

---

²   Aramaic for 'Jesus'. I'll explain later.

2. Biblical scholarship has reached a new high in recent decades

As I said, earlier generations were unwilling to challenge the Bible from a scientific or historical point of view, but now we *are* willing, and, moreover, we can. Biblical scholarship has reached a new high in recent decades. New and better evidence has become available for historians, theologians, archaeologists and linguists to scrutinise for factual accuracy and new meanings. They have a better understanding of 1st Century Palestinian society than ever before.

Scholars go back to the earliest possible sources to reveal the influence of the numerous editors and translators. They can discern with a high degree of certainty where sections have been added or where original material has been altered. They examine the style and language of different passages to identify where several authors were at work. They study the context in which the manuscripts were written so they can piece together clues and fill in the gaps.

Much of what follows here has been known for at least a couple of centuries and taught in seminaries and theological colleges around the world. Some has found a wider platform in the broadcast media and literature, but is rarely communicated to the people in the pews.

3. The clergy knows the truth, but the faithful don't want to hear it!

I've had many conversations with churchmen and women in recent years and discovered that many of them continue to teach the same old things without really believing it themselves, but they dare not say so for fear of confusing their congregations and losing their employment. One Anglican vicar told me that, like all trainee clergy, she had studied the Bible from a factual-historical point of view at university. I asked her why, then, vicars continued to peddle the same old line in their Sunday sermons as if nothing had moved on from the 17th or 18th Centuries. Her reply astounded me. *'Because they (the congregation) don't want to hear it!'*

'Because they don't want to hear it!' Why not? Psychologists tell us that once people have made up their minds about something they don't want to change so I don't expect to make any friends in church circles by presenting these facts. Previously I had believed that the church[3] itself was the sticking point, being suspicious of any knowledge that could make its traditional beliefs redundant and threaten the foundations of its faith. Once an idea has been labelled 'the word' or 'will' of the Almighty and people have convinced themselves that this is so, all discretion, all criticism, all scrutiny goes out of the window. For example, if you believe that the gospels were written by contemporaries of 'Jesus' who knew him personally and wrote down what they observed at the time, then no amount of evidence and reason can shake your faith in them. Your mind closes to alternative ideas, and so do your ears. Common sense flies out of the window. But surely any belief system that cannot survive scrutiny is of little value?

This book offers a selection of facts which I hope you, the reader, will find interesting and significant. It may change your viewpoint on certain things, or not – your choice. I'm confident that few independent experts on the history and practice of Christianity would disagree with the information presented here, although some may differ with my interpretation. All I can do is set out the facts in good faith according to my understanding. Here goes!

---

[3]   When I write of 'the church', I am referring generally to the ruling bodies that dictate doctrine, policy and procedure and the clergy who preach it.

4. Jesus' wasn't called 'Jesus'

The first and most obvious thing about the main character of the gospels is that he wasn't called 'Jesus', nor was his surname 'Christ'. He was probably known to his family and friends by the Aramaic[4] name Yeshua bar Yehosef – Yeshua Son of Joseph (or Yeshua ben Josef in Hebrew). Jesus is the Greek equivalent. So why Greek? All the books of the New Testament were originally written in Greek, not Hebrew or Latin as commonly supposed. Then around 382 CE[5], a priest called Jerome began translating the New Testament scripts into Latin and decided to stay with Yeshua's Greek name. It stuck even though as far as we know Yeshua didn't speak Greek and neither did his disciples.

After his death, Yeshua became known as 'the Christ' at the instigation of his leading apostle, Paul of Tarsus. The literal meaning of Christ is 'the anointed one', from the Greek 'Christos'. 'Messiah' means much the same thing. Yeshua is better known to the world as 'Jesus Christ', but he would not have answered to either name during his lifetime. Strange, isn't it? Millions of subscribers to the world's largest and most influential religion refer to their Lord and Saviour by a name he would not have recognised! So, with due deference, I will refer to him as Yeshua throughout this book, and the resurrected Yeshua as 'Christ or the Christ'.

---

[4]   A dialect of Hebrew (now defunct) once spoken in Northern Palestine, and Yeshua's mother tongue.

[5]   I prefer CE (Common Era) and BCE (Before Common Era) to AD and BC because they are more accurate.

5. Yeshua bar Yehosef was barely mentioned by the chroniclers of his time

Did Yeshua bar Yehosef actually exist? At one time I doubted it. I placed him in the same category as King Arthur, Hercules and Robin Hood, mythical characters only loosely based on real people. But now I'm sure he did, even though the historical evidence is slim. The problem is, the New Testament texts and most of the so-called Gnostic Gospels[6] were all written by men who never met Yeshua and were intent on glorifying him. They are the only documentary sources from his century that place any importance on him. He is central to the gospels, which were, after all, created to tell his story, but from a historical perspective he was a marginal figure, barely worthy of a mention by the major chroniclers of the time.

6. If there is a supreme intelligence, it doesn't matter what you call it

I do not intend to discuss the existence or otherwise of God here for this is a matter of belief that can't be proved or disproved either way. For the record, I do believe there is a supreme intelligence, an omnipresent energy and information field that underpins everything. I believe science is getting closer to understanding it, and I'll give more clues at the end of this book. I also believe that it doesn't matter what you call it. The Hebrew Scriptures called it Elohim, YHWH[7] and Jehovah, but Jews, the 'chosen people', were forbidden to utter these names. Yeshua believed he had a personal relationship with the deity so intense, so intimate that he

---

[6]   A handful of documents among those rejected for inclusion in the New Testament at the time it was compiled by the Roman authorities (382 CE).

[7]   Pronounced Yar-way.

called it 'Abba' (Father). For him, 'Abba' was as real as the people and animals around him.

Again with due deference I shall respect the Hebrew tradition by refer to the Jewish and Christian deity as 'G_d'. Masculine pronouns he, him, his and so on are normally used to signify G_d although strictly speaking 'he' doesn't have a gender in which case we should refer to 'him' as 'it'. For the rest of this book, that's what I'll do. If you are uncomfortable with calling G-d 'it', I suggest you reflect on your religious programming.

7. If we want a rounded picture, we must be look at all available sources

Church theologians say that everything we need to know about Yeshua can be found in the New Testament, and that what is written there is all true. But surely if we want a rounded picture, we must be look at *all* available sources. That's not easy; Yeshua barely features in any non-Christian sources from the 1st Century and none at all from the first third of that century when he was alive.

Outside the gospels there are only four known references to him, and they don't say very much:

- Flavius Josephus[8], a pro-Roman Jewish historian (c37-c100 CE), referred to him as a 'Yeshua who was called Christ', a healer from Galilee[9] who attracted large crowds, told stories and was put to death because he made the authorities nervous.

---

[8] Antt.20, 197-203 = XX, 9,1)
[9] A small province that is now part of Northern Israel.

- The Roman historian Tacitus (c55–c120 CE) wrote of the 'Chrestiani' blamed by the Emperor Nero for setting fire to Rome in 64 CE. The name derived from 'Christus' who 'was executed in the reign of Tiberius on the orders of the procurator Pontius Pilate' for allegedly refusing to pay taxes to the Emperor.'[10] Tacitus tells us that ten years after Yeshua's death around 30 CE the authorities were aware of conflict in Rome's Jewish community about whether Yeshua had really been their Messiah. Christians (or 'People of the Way' as they were known at that time) were mistrusted by mainstream Jews, persecuted by Emperor Nero and widely mocked.
- Gaius Suetonius Tranquillus (c75–150 CE), a Roman biographer and historian[11], and Pliny the Younger (c62–113 CE)[12] also mention conflicts between Yeshua's followers and the authorities.

Neither Josephus, Tacitus, Tranquillus nor Pliny considered Yeshua's teachings worth a mention, and none verify the most extraordinary events described in the New Testament, the virgin birth, miracles, resurrection and ascension.

Historians have long expressed amazement that a man who, according to the gospel authors, was mobbed by crowds, performed miracles and returned from the dead didn't get much of a mention in any of the non-devotional literature of the time, whether Jewish, Roman, Greek, or whatever. It suggests he was a fairly minor figure during his lifetime, almost unknown outside his own region, and that much of what was written about him came from the creative imagination of a tiny group of people - the Christian community.

---

[10]   Annals XV, 44,3)
[11]   Claudius, 25
[12]   Epistles X, 96

8. Yeshua was born between 6 and 4 BCE

We will never know the precise date of Yeshua's birth but there are convincing reasons to believe that it fell within 6 to 4 BCE since the gospels say that the old King Herod was still alive, and he died in 4 BCE. The traditional calendar that dated Yeshua's birth at the year zero, designated the years since as AD (Anno Domini – the year of our Lord) and the years before as BC (before Christ) was based on an error. CE (Common Era – year zero and after) and BCE (Before Common Era) are more correct.

Yeshua lived for around 35 years; most authorities date his death at around 30 CE or a year or two either way. That doesn't sound much these days but was a fairly typical lifespan in Palestine in those days.

9. Yeshua lived in 'interesting' times

There's an ancient Chinese curse, 'May you live in interesting times.' Yeshua certainly did, and we know a great deal about them. No other place and time in history has been as widely studied as Palestine in the 1st Century.

Palestine was, as now, a land under brutal occupation. Yeshua's people, the Jews, were suppressed not only by the Romans, but also a puppet administration headed by the tyrannical King Herod 'the Great' who paid lip service to his people while dancing to the tune of his foreign paymasters. Herod was so reviled that when he died in 4 BCE his subjects petitioned the Roman emperor for a change of government, but to no avail. Instead, the emperor divided the land into three and gave each of Herod's sons governance of a province. The most northerly, Galilee, was granted to Herod Antipas, a much hated and rather stupid ruler who had nothing but contempt for his subjects, but as long as he kept the peace and paid his taxes the Romans left him alone. Each town and village in Galilee was ruled by a council of local Jews, but there was always a Roman garrison nearby in case of trouble.

Galilee was largely rural and impoverished. It was looked down upon by the sophisticates in Jerusalem, the headquarters of Judaism eighty miles to the south. Jerusalem was the capital of the province of Judea, which passed to another of Herod's sons. He proved so incompetent the emperor quickly replaced him with a Roman Prefect.

For centuries the Jewish people had desperately awaited the coming of a 'Messiah' to lead them to freedom, by force if necessary. They believed this was prophesised in the ancient scriptures, and many thought this imminent. Hopes had been raised a century and a half earlier when a popular freedom fighter, Judas Maccabeus, had briefly wrested control from the Romans and established a degree of independence, but they were dashed when the emperor sent troops to invade and re-establish their dominance.

The lives of ordinary Jews were blighted by another powerful group, the religious authorities in Jerusalem. They oversaw a set of restrictions on the populace enshrined in the Torah (Hebrew Law). At the heart of the Torah were the Purity Laws which were believed to align the Jewish people with the will of YHWH, their one true god.

It was into this impoverished, subjugated and embittered land that Yeshua was born.

10. Holiness was equated with purity in Jewish society

In Jewish society at that time, holiness was equated with cleanliness and governed by the Purity Laws which dated back to the Torah written hundreds of years before. Strict Jews carried out hundreds of ritual duties every day, believing that they would elevate themselves above the common man and secure eternal life and glory for themselves. Among the 613 strictures of the Torah were:

- Not to wear clothing of the opposite sex.
- To circumcise all males on the eight day after birth.
- Not to withhold food, clothing, and sexual relations from your wife.
- Not to have sexual relations with an animal.
- Not to have homosexual relations.
- Not to marry non-Jews.
- To ritually slaughter an animal before eating it.
- Not to work the land during the seventh year.
- Not to tear priestly garments.
- Not to appear at the temple without offerings.
- Not to listen to a false prophet.
- Not to possess inaccurate scales or weights even if not for use.
- To fear and respect your father and mother, and not to curse or strike them.
- Not to panic or retreat during battle.

Purity depended on:

- Birth. The priests and Levites (which were both hereditary positions) were the most pure, followed by the rest of the Jewish born population, then converts. Near the bottom were those born out of wedlock, homosexuals and, right at the bottom, those without a penis (yes, really!). All non-Jews were considered impure, including the Romans and the hated Samaritans.

- Gender. Women were thought to be less pure than men due to childbirth and menstruation, but being male did not automatically make you pure.
- Behaviour. The unclean included criminals, outcasts and untouchables. Jews often used the word 'sinner' to denote impure.
- Physical wellness. The chronically ill and maimed were impure; so were people lacking in personal hygiene and those with damaged testicles.
- Wealth: being rich did not automatically make you pure, but poverty made you impure. Since the poor could not afford to observe the purity laws, it indicated unrighteous living.

11. The Purity System was centred on the Jerusalem Temple

The Purity System created a society with sharp social boundaries, centred on the Jerusalem Temple. The priesthood relied on it to maintain their high social, economic and religious status. The impure (the majority) were excluded from entering the Temple Mount area. Everything was classified according to its degree of purity. Agricultural produce, for instance, could not be pronounced clean until a tithe had been paid to the priests – for them, a nice little earner!

The gospels tell us that Yeshua had an alternative social vision in which love, compassion and humility replaced purity as the guiding principles. Yet it is still with us, but in a different form. How you speak, your taste in clothes, music, art, food, hairstyle, perfume, youthfulness, fashionable appearance are all signs of 'purity' of a sort. People still judge by wealth and status and there's as much prejudice as ever there was. Except it's more subtle.

THE HEBREW SCRIPTURES

12. The Hebrew Scriptures were Yeshua's inspiration

The Christian religion has two main foundations: the Holy Scriptures as presented in the Bible, and the interpretations of church theologians filling in the gaps in Biblical teachings as they perceived them. Christianity depends heavily on the Bible, so it's important to understand how it came to be written and how its two major parts, the Hebrew Scriptures (the correct name for the Old Testament)[13] and the New Testament relate to each other.

You won't find everything that Christians believe and practise in the Bible. Many of the church's teachings do not date from Yeshua's time nor even the decades when the New Testament was written. It has nothing to say on many issues (e.g. homosexuality, celibacy and contraception) so in the 4th Century, following the Roman 'conversion', the church assumed the authority to expand on Biblical teachings where 'gaps' existed. Much church practice and doctrine developed around this time.

---

[13]   Jews don't recognise the New Testament, so the Old Testament is their Bible.

13. The Hebrew Scriptures were the original Christian canon

The Hebrew Scriptures were the original Christian canon. They make up more than three-quarters of the Christian Bible. Many Christians think the only relevance of the Hebrew Scriptures is that they prophesy Yeshua's birth and Messiah-ship, but as we shall see, this is a fallacy.

The New Testament writings repeatedly demonstrate that Yeshua was thoroughly grounded in the Hebrew Scriptures. They were the source of his inspiration; they created the culture into which he was born, regulated his day to day activities and shaped his thinking. For example, nowhere in the gospels does Yeshua reject the Jewish custom of circumcision as prescribed in Jewish Law, unlike Paul of Tarsus and the author of Acts of the Apostles who considered it irrelevant.

The New Testament could not exist in isolation; without the Hebrew Scriptures it wouldn't even make sense. So if you think it was a replacement for the Hebrew Scriptures, that made them obsolete, think again. Unless we acknowledge this in full, we will never understanding Yeshua.

14. It took eight hundred years to write the Hebrew Scriptures

The Hebrew Bible is a collection of thirty-nine books, arranged in three sections – the Torah or Pentateuch (Law or Teaching), Prophets and Writings[14]. It was written over a period of eight hundred years and gives an account of the history of the Jewish people over approximately fifteen hundred years. The last book,

---

[14]   The Apocrypha which appears in the Roman Catholic Bible has another twelve books, but they are not recognised as part of the Hebrew Scriptures.

Daniel, was completed only one hundred and fifty years or so before the birth of Yeshua, and the definitive list of books to be included was only agreed by the Jewish religious leaders around 90 BCE.

No-one really knows who wrote the Hebrew Scriptures, although we can be confident that we know who *didn't* write it; for instance, according to Jewish tradition, the revered prophet Moses wrote the first five books of the Bible, the Torah[15], around 1300 BCE, but we can't even be certain that Moses existed outside of Jewish folklore. Scholars today believe that the Torah is more likely to have been compiled by a variety of authors between the 8th and 5th Centuries BCE.

Interestingly for most of this time the Hebrews did not just believe in one G-d, just that theirs was the best. Whenever they were tempted to worship other gods, they believed, the one true G_d punish them until they mended their ways. Then all sorts of good things would flow.

15. Five 'writers' or 'traditions' contributed to the Torah

By analysing the styles, language and ideas in the Torah, scholars have identified five 'writers' or 'traditions' who contributed to its composition:

> J - the Yahwist source, so called because the writer refers to G_d as YHWH (Yahweh[16]) or Jehovah. These are the oldest writings, around 950-750 BCE. The J texts include the second creation

---

[15]   Also known as the Pentateuch.
[16]   Pronounced Yar-way.

story (Adam and Eve in the Garden of Eden) and Cain and Abel.

E – the Elohist source, written around 850-800 BCE, uses the word Elohim for G_d. The E texts include the stories of Abraham and Isaac, Deborah and Jacob.

D the Deuteronomist, dating from around 700-600 BCE. D describes the covenant between Jehovah and his people and the cycle of blessing, disobedience, punishment, and redemption which followed over many generations.

P – the Priestly source, written around 550-500 BCE, includes the first creation story (in the opening passages of Genesis)[17], Noah's flood, Jacob and Esau, the Hebrews' escape from Egypt and the Ten Commandments. P formalised the ritualistic laws which formed the background to Yeshua's skirmishes with the Pharisees[18] in the New Testament.

R - the Redactor or 'editor/combiner,' working around 400 BCE. There may have been more than one; indeed this is highly probable. R edited the original texts to remove some of the discrepancies between his sources and made some additions, but we don't know if 'he' took anything out.

---

[17]   Please note, the first creation story in Genesis is 300-400 years more recent than the second.

[18]   A strict religious sect who saw themselves as protectors of Jewish Law and believed it should be observed to the letter.

As for the Prophets and the Writings, the evidence of authorship is just as shaky. Most were probably passed on orally for centuries until being written down around 400 to 90 BCE. We can be fairly sure that, contrary to popular belief, the great King David didn't write most of the Psalms and King Solomon didn't write Proverbs or Song of Solomon. As for Job, Ecclesiastes, Jonah and the rest – nobody knows.

16. The Hebrew Scriptures are full of inaccuracies and contradictions

We don't have to look beyond the opening pages to find the first significant contradiction in the Bible. In the very first chapter of Genesis, G_d creates the sky, the earth, vegetation and the sun and moon in the first four days (curiously the waters already existed); aquatic creatures and birds on the fifth day; land creatures and finally men and women on the sixth. These nameless humans are given dominion[19] over the earth. Then G_d rests on the seventh[20].

In the second chapter, the earth, heavens and the first man, Adam[21], are created on the same day, then a beautiful garden, the Garden of Eden, for Adam's home. Living creatures are created to keep Adam company, and finally a companion and helper for Adam, Eve. There's no mention of six or seven days. I reiterate: in Chapter One, man and woman are created simultaneously as G_d's final flourish; in Chapter Two, the man is created before the animals, and the woman later as an afterthought.

---

[19] Dominion can be misread as the right to do what you want and has been used as an excuse for all manner of cruelty to G_d's creatures. A better word would be stewardship, which implies caring, working with, with respect for creation.

[20] G_d's day of rest was later seen as the justification for complete inactivity on the Jewish Sabbath.

[21] Originally Adham, Hebrew for 'man'.

If anyone tries to convince you that the creation stories are literally true, ask them 'which story?' They cannot both be true! But the church papers over the cracks. In my churchgoing years I never heard these two stories read together and compared. No-one ever pointed out the contradictions, nor did anyone seem bothered by them, probably because, like me, they hadn't noticed.

So why the difference? It's because the two stories come from separate sources, 'J' and 'P', written more than three hundred years apart and later combined into a single narrative, probably by the Redactor, 'R'. The 'P' version was probably written in the 6th Century BCE around the time when the Jews were exiled in Babylon. Scholars debate what it meant in that setting. And that's just for starters. If Adam and Eve were the first humans, where did Cain and Abel, their sons', wives come from? If everyone apart from Noah and his family perished in a great flood when they took to the Ark[22], then surely Noah, not Adam, is the father of humankind? And was he really 600 years old? As Oxford Professor Diarmaid MacCullough, an expert on biblical history, wrote: 'The chronology of the Book of Genesis simply does not add up as a historical narrative when it is placed in a reliably historical context'[23].

As for the rest of the Hebrew Scriptures, some passages are based on verifiable historical truth, such as the exile, enslavement and return of the Jewish people by the Babylonians around 600-500 BCE, but others have no basis in fact. For example, there is no written or archaeological evidence that the Egyptians ever enslaved the Hebrews (as reported in the Book of Exodus), nor that a large group of Hebrews (or any other tribe) wandered in

---

[22]   Genesis, Chapters 6 and 7.

[23]   In *A History of Christianity*.

the desert for forty years before conquering the 'Promised Land'[24]. This is based on events that almost certainly never happened; indeed, there is no evidence that any of the events described in the Pentateuch are literally true.

17. 'Truth' does not have to be 'true'

The Hebrew Bible is largely a symbolic and highly fictionalised account of a people's struggles and their attempt to understand their world. Even so, stories can contain an element of 'truth' without being literally 'true' – that's the appeal of Aesop, Homer, the Brothers Grimm and almost every great novelist and playwright. Perhaps the ancient biblical writers were not so much concerned with *facts* as *meaning*, and it would be more beneficial to ask ourselves, 'What *meaning* were they seeking to convey?' than, 'Is this literally true?'

---

[24]   Justification for the founding of the State of Israel in 1948 is based on these legends.

THE NEW TESTAMENT

18. All reported speech in the New Testament is only an interpretation of what was actually said

As we've already observed, the entire New Testament was originally written in Greek - a language that Yeshua and his disciples barely knew. Their everyday tongue was Galilean Aramaic. He may have understood a smattering of marketplace Greek since Sepphoris, the capital of Galilee and just a stone's throw from Nazareth, was on the main trade route from Greece to Egypt and Asia Minor and it's possible he heard it spoken.

Most Jews also learned Hebrew so they could understand the scriptures, just as Moslems today learn Arabic to read the Qu'ran. Yeshua would also have needed Hebrew to communicate with the temple dignitaries in Jerusalem who would surely not have spoken Aramaic. We don't know if he spoke Latin, the language of the Romans. Probably not, which poses an interesting question – how did he communicate with Pontius Pilate, the Roman Prefect, if indeed he did?[25]

The implications are profound. Since the entire New Testament was written in a language foreign to Yeshua and his associates, all

---

[25]   See my comments on the trial narratives, page xxx

reported speech in the gospels must be at least a third- or fourth-hand translation of what was actually said. Or, more accurately, of *the authors' impressions of what was said or what the authors would have wanted him to say.* Moreover, Aramaic, Hebrew and ancient Greek are said to be extremely difficult to translate into modern languages. Fortunately today's experts have a better knowledge of these ancient languages and the people who spoke them than ever before, so modern translations are considerably more accurate than their predecessors. Scholars have thrown such additional light upon the original meaning of the scriptures that we cannot assume that a single paragraph of the Bible is understood in our day as it was intended at the time it was written.

Here's the key. *When reading any Bible passage we should ask ourselves, 'What meaning did these events and sayings have for people living in that place at that time?'* Then look for the *meaning* behind the words.

19. The King James Bible was the best English translation available, but is no longer

A good example is the King James Version of the Bible much beloved in English speaking countries. It was published in 1611, roughly when William Shakespeare wrote Macbeth, and was the best English translation available at the time. It is still widely used. It was based on a version produced by the Dutch scholar, Erasmus (1466 – 1536). He didn't attempt to go back to the earliest texts, but relied on hand-written copies of copies passed down through generations of scribes. But nowadays its language is difficult to understand and we know it is not always true to the 1st Century authors' intentions.

Some recent editions of the New Testament have merely changed the King James Bible into modern language, but the best versions go back to the oldest possible sources to uncover the meaning intended by the authors. Since there are now much better and more accurate translations, surely the King James Bible should be consigned to history and read in the same spirit as we would read Shakespeare or Chaucer.

20. The content of the New Testament was only finalised in 382 CE

We tend to think of the New Testament as a book, or at least, part of a larger book (the Bible), but it was not written in this form. It was originally separate manuscripts hand-written on papyrus or leather scrolls, and copied by hand. They circulated for around three hundred years until in 382 CE church leaders in Rome agreed which 27 texts should make up the official New Testament. It was then added to the Hebrew Scriptures to create the Christian Bible.

Chronology
(Best estimates by leading scholars)
6-4 BCE Yeshua born.

10 CE Paul of Tarsus born.

27-28 CE John the Baptists preaches.

29/30 CE Execution of John the Baptist

c30 CE The crucifixion.

36-40 CE Paul's vision on the road to Damascus

47 CE The word 'Christian' coined in Antioch (an early church).

47-56 CE Missionary journeys of Paul.

50-80 CE Gospel of Thomas

52-90 CE Letters attributed to Paul

64-67 Paul taken prisoner by Roman government

(under Emperor Nero) and executed.

65-70 CE Letter to the Hebrews

68-69 Cephas said to be executed in Rome.

68-75 CE Gospel of 'Mark'

80-90 CE Gospel of 'Matthew'

80-90 CE Gospel of 'Luke'

80-95 Acts of the Apostles.

80-100 CE Letters of James, 1 Peter, John and Jude written.

95-105 CE Gospel of 'John'

90-100 CE Book of Revelation written.

100 CE First collection of Paul's letters compiled.

125 CE 2nd letter of Peter written.

Chronology cont.

(Best estimates by leading scholars)

200 CE Bishop of Rome first recognised as Pope.

313 CE Emperor Constantine makes Christianity the official religion of the Roman Empire (Edict of Milan).

325 CE First Council of Nicaea.

382 CE Church leaders in Rome recognise today's 27 books as the New Testament.

451 CE Council of Chalcedon ruled on the human and divine nature of Yeshua.

21. The earliest passages in the New Testament are in the seven letters of Paul of Tarsus

The earliest passages in the New Testament appear in letters written by the apostle Paul of Tarsus around 52 CE. They predate the first gospel, 'Mark', by 15-20 years. They are important because the Christian community had been heavily influenced by Paul's views by the time the official gospels came to be written (between 70 CE and 105 CE). Paul's genuine letters are the only New Testament writings of a known individual describing his experiences first hand. This cannot be said of any of the others, including the gospels and Acts of the Apostles.

Thirteen letters in Paul's name appear in the New Testament. Paul wrote, or more accurately, dictated, seven of them; the other six were not written by him; they are forgeries, made, presumably, by Paul's followers and successors. Some of the early letters probably reached their final form several decades after his death[26].

'Paul's' letters are arranged in the New Testament according to length, the longest (Romans) first and shortest (Philemon) last. This is not in the order in which they were written, nor does it reflect their authenticity, subject matter, literary quality or importance.

The seven definitely written (or, more accurately, dictated) by him, all between 52-62 CE, are:

- Thessalonians 1
- Philippians
- Philemon
- Corinthians 1
- Corinthians 2

---

[26] See Kenneth Davis, 'Don't Know Much About The Bible.'

- Galatians
- Romans

Four letters are so different in style, content and doctrine and written so late that they could not have been by the same man:

- Ephesians (80-100 CE)
- Timothy 1 (95-100 CE)
- Timothy 2 (95-100 CE)
- Titus (95-100 CE)

Colossians and Thessalonians 2 are also attributed to Paul, but scholars are divided about their authenticity. The consensus is they were probably written in the seventh or eighth decades.

Forgeries? Yes, but in those days it was considered perfectly acceptable to use the name of a respected deceased person, either to add authority to a document or express what the writer thought he *would* have said had he still been alive.

22. The New Testament letters justify slavery

Paul's letters have been used to support many things, among them misogyny, sexual abstention, gender inequality, self-flagellation (more of these later) and slavery. Keeping slaves was a common practice in Greek and Roman society, and the coming of Christianity made little difference.

There are several references in the New Testament that appear to accept it. For example, in Paul's letter to Philemon (which was actually written by him) he pleads with the addressee to take back a former slave 'no longer as a slave but as ..... a beloved brother.'[27]

---

[27]   Philemon 15-16

The author of the First Letter of Peter urged Christian slaves to accept the authority of their masters with all deference and take whatever punishment they were handed out whether they had 'earned' it or not[28]. Neither letter said that slavery was wrong.

These letters were widely used to justify slavery, especially the kind of racial slavery seen in the Americas and Caribbean in the 17th, 18th and 19th Centuries where it was used to advance European economic interests. Thankfully slavery is not sanctioned in most Christian countries today, but it has never been entirely eliminated and still has its apologists in some Christian circles.

23. Around 100 CE some of Paul's letters were compiled into a single document

Around 100 CE, shortly after the letters to Timothy and Titus were written, some of Paul's letters were compiled into a single document. These later found their way into the New Testament.

Paul's letters were addressed to named audiences on specific subjects and were not intended for publication. He would probably be amazed that people are still reading them today, especially since, like Yeshua and his disciples, he thought the known world was about to end[29]. They contain some of the most exquisite passages ever written, such as his reflections on love in his First Letter to the Corinthians. If you've never read this, I urge you to do so; it's beautiful.[30]

Paul must have produced many writings subsequently lost or discarded, since some of the surviving letters read like one side

---

[28] 1 Peter 2: 18-24
[29] More of this later.
[30] 1 Corinthians 13:1-13

of an ongoing debate, like listening to a person on the telephone without hearing the person at the other end. We can only speculate on what these had to say.

24. Paul is the only New Testament author whose adult life overlapped with Yeshua's

There is no record of Paul and Yeshua meeting, although Paul is the only New Testament author whose adult life overlapped with Yeshua's. Paul's letters show little interest in Yeshua the man; they barely refer to his life and teachings, he quotes not a single parable or saying, and makes no mention of Yeshua's birth.

It's hard to imagine Yeshua's leading apostle having no interest in him, especially since he visited Jerusalem and met up with at least two of Yeshua's disciples. It's just that there's no written evidence that he showed any interest.

25. 'Gospel' means 'good news'

'Gospel' means 'good news'. There are four in the New Testament, carefully selected by the Roman authorities in the 4th Century from the hundreds available. These are the 'official' gospels, sanctioned by the Roman church and state and widely read ever since. There were other gospels too, such as the so-called 'Gnostic Gospels', but these did not make it into the New Testament.

The first three, 'Mark', 'Matthew' and 'Luke', are known as the Synoptic Gospels because they present a similar view of Yeshua's ministry. The Second and Third ('Matthew' and 'Luke') used the First ('Mark') as their main source and added extra material of their own. The Fourth, 'John', is very different, as we shall see. Each gospel writer had his own point of view. Reading between the lines tells us a great deal about the authors and the communities from which they came.

26. Names were not ascribed to the gospels until the middle of the 2nd Century

As a child I was told that the gospels and Acts of the Apostles were written by eye witnesses to the events they described, and that the New Testament letters were all written by the men whose names they bear. I was also told that John's Gospel, three of the New Testament letters and Revelation were all written by Yeshua's disciple John. I suspect most people brought up as Christians are told the same.

As I surveyed the literature on Christianity, I found numerous statements such as this (I paraphrase slightly):

> 'The New Testament is made up entirely of documents written by Yeshua's apostles – men who had unparalleled access to him and his teaching – or under the immediate direction of the apostles. The only exceptions are Tiago (later known as James) and Jude, who were Yeshua's own brothers.'[31]

This is simply not true! For a start, the gospels were written at least forty years after Yeshua's death in a language they did not speak and presuppose knowledge that the apostles did not have. They also refer to events that had not yet happened at the time the apostles were alive, such as the ransacking of Jerusalem by the Romans in 70 CE. The fact is, authors' names were not ascribed to the gospels until the middle of the 2nd Century, when eye

---

[31] Rico Tice and Barry Cooper, *Christianity Explored*, p124-125

witnesses were long dead. The names Mark, Matthew, Luke and John undoubtedly belonged to real people, but this does not mean that these real people were the genuine authors. Besides, all the gospels were later edited and added to by persons unknown before reaching their final form.

27. Neither Yeshua or his twelve closest disciples left any writings

The gospels say that Yeshua spoke to thousands of people during his ministry, but as far as we know neither he nor his closest disciples left any writings. Probably no-one who heard him speak did either; if they did, they are long since lost, as are all the original manuscripts.

The Fourth Gospel says that Yeshua made a few jottings in the mud[32], so he could write, but apart from Levi the tax collector the disciples were almost certainly illiterate. They were simple folk, mainly peasants and fishermen, and it would have been extraordinary if any of them had learned to write in their own language let alone polished Greek! Perhaps Yeshua didn't think there was much point in writing anything down since, as we shall see, he believed the world as he knew it was about to end. It was far more urgent to spread his message to the uneducated poor by word of mouth.

28. The official gospels depended on stories passed on by word of mouth for several generations before being written down

Some Bible scholars believe that a collection of Yeshua's sayings was compiled into a manuscript known as 'The Book of Q' (Quelle) after his death. They point to similarities in the Synoptic

---

[32] John 8:8

Gospels which suggest that they came from a common source, although there is a better explanation, that 'Matthew' and 'Luke' copied from 'Mark'. Q exists only in theory; no-one has ever seen a copy and it is unlikely that one will ever turn up.

Some of the writings discovered near Qumran on the Dead Sea (in modern Israel) between 1947 and 1956, also contain sayings attributed to Yeshua (notably the gnostic 'Gospel of Thomas'). Some believe that there was also a 'Book of Signs' which described miracles which Yeshua performed to prove that he was the Son of G_d, and which formed a substantial chunk of the Fourth Gospel[33]. But like Q, the evidence is circumstantial and no copies have survived the centuries.

Unless Q, the Book of Signs and/or similar documents actually existed, the original versions of the official gospels depended on stories and sayings passed on by word of mouth for several generations before being committed to parchment. None of the original manuscripts has survived, so scholars use deductive logic to work out what the originals contained. But we know for certain that they have been amended, translated, mistranslated and copied by hand many times before reaching the forms we see today.

29. The Gnostics formed an alternative branch of the new religion

We know that hundreds of 'gospels' were rejected as the Roman authorities deliberated over their final choice towards the end of the 4th Century. Many were excluded because they did not accord with the officially approved view. Although some of the rejected texts remained in circulation for several centuries, most early

---

[33]   John 1:19 to 12:50.

Christian writings were lost. Many were deliberately destroyed, and others were simply allowed to disappear.

Among the rejects were a collection of writings known as the Gnostic Gospels. The Gnostics formed an alternative branch of the new religion in the decades following the crucifixion. While official church thinking largely came to reflect the views of the Apostle Paul, that faith in Yeshua's death and resurrection lay at the heart of Christianity, the Gnostics believed that G_d must be found through knowledge of truth and practising what one knows.[34]

Gnostic writings depict Yeshua as purely divine, his human body being a mere illusion. They saw him this way because they regarded matter as evil, and therefore believed that a divine spirit would never have taken on a material body. Yeshua's teachings could help one get closer to G_d, but were no substitute for personal experience. Indeed, according to the Gospel of Thomas, when a disciple achieves enlightenment, Yeshua is no longer his or her Master because the two have become equal. Furthermore, the Gnostics resisted authoritarian structures, which was hardly likely to be popular with the Roman authorities.

It was only natural for the official church to do everything it could to suppress them and they were largely successful. But they could not write them out of history.

30. There is no mention of Yeshua in the Dead Sea Scrolls

Some of the Gnostic writings lay hidden for centuries until unearthed in the 1940s and 50s at Qumran as part of the collection known as the Dead Sea Scrolls. Most are little more than fragments. Experts have patiently pieced them together and

---

[34] The word 'Agnostic' (ag-gnostic) came to mean one who does not know.

found they include some of the oldest known versions of the Hebrew Scriptures. There is no mention of Yeshua, Pilate or Herod in the Qumran scrolls, but they say a great deal about the political and religious turmoil of the time. They confirm that life was at life was not all sweetness and light for the 'People of the Way' in the second half of the 1st Century.

When the Dead Sea Scrolls first came to light, the Catholic Church tried to suppress them. When knowledge of them leaked out, they tried to discredit them. They did not want them to be circulated then, and are no keener for them to be circulated now!

31. The most notable Gnostic Gospels are the Gospels of Thomas, Philip and Mary Magdalene

The Gospel of Thomas is the most noteworthy Gnostic text. It contains 114 sayings, many of which are remarkably similar to words attributed to Yeshua in the Synoptics.

The Gospel of Philip is shorter and more controversial. In one fragment, it states that Mary Magdalene was Yeshua's favourite disciple and he often kissed her on the mouth. It led to a great deal of speculation about their relationship!

Fragments of the Gospel of Mary Magdalene were discovered in the 1890's but published only after the Second World War. Experts date it as 2nd Century so it cannot have been written by her. Controversially it portrays her as a strong and wise leader, in contrast to the 'official' gospels which portray her as a woman who was possessed by demons until Yeshua exorcised them. She is often unfairly described as a prostitute, although there's not a single sentence in the New Testament that links her with prostitution.

The existence of the Gnostic Gospels confirms that there once was much more early written material to choose from than is available to us now. No-one knows for sure what manuscripts were lost and what they said about Yeshua, the Christ and the early church.

32. 70 CE was a watershed year for the Christian religion

Forty years after Yeshua's death, the Jewish world was shaken to the core by a cataclysmic event. The Emperor of Rome sent a huge army to Jerusalem to crush an armed rebellion by the Jews. After a five month siege the walls were reduced to rubble, the city ransacked, and the great Temple that had stood for a thousand years destroyed. According to the contemporary historian, Josephus, over a million Jews were killed and 95,000 taken as prisoners, and the fortunate ones fled to the hills.

Prior to 70 CE, Jerusalem had hosted a small Christian community headed by Yeshua's brother Tiago (a.k.a. James). This disappeared, and subsequently no Christian community existed in the city for 300 years. As we shall see, the New Testament writings can be easily identified as pre- or post-70 CE; most were written *after* this date.

THE NEW TESTAMENT GOSPELS

33. The First Gospel, 'Mark', was written around or soon after 70 CE.

'Mark's' was the first of the four official gospels to be written[35], around or soon after 70 CE. Only Paul's genuine letters and the letter to the Hebrews were written before this, which means ninety percent of the New Testament was written after. The author seems to have been aware that Jerusalem had been destroyed and was offering hope to his fellow Christians[36].

Nobody knows who wrote it. The author makes no claims in the text to being an eyewitness. Some have suggested that it was written by a young disciple of Cephas; if this were true, he would be author closest to Yeshua, but it's unlikely. Others think it could have been written by a young companion of Paul, John-Mark, before until they quarrelled and went their separate ways (Paul seemed to fall out with a lot of people!), but this is unlikely too.

Some think it was written in Syria, others in Rome. There are no indications that the author was familiar with the geography of Palestine. It seems to have been written for gentile[37] Christians,

---

[35] Although in sequence it follows the Second Gospel, Matthew, in the New Testament.

[36] All three Synoptic Gospels claimed that Yeshua had prophesised the destruction of Jerusalem, but did he? We can't be sure. Since all the gospels were written *after* 70 CE, it is possible that some retrospective prophesising took place. The second part of the 'prophecy', that he would rebuild it in three days, clearly did not materialise, because it's still a ruin!

[37] i.e. non-Jewish

since the author, probably Jewish, felt the need to explain Jewish law and customs.

34. There is no birth story in the First Gospel, nor did the original text claim that a resurrection had taken place

'Mark's' gospel begins with Yeshua's submersion in the River Jordan by John the Baptist and ends with a group of women discovering the empty tomb. There is no divine conception, no birth story, no shepherds, wise men or flight into Egypt[38]. Nor did the original text make a definitive statement that a resurrection had taken place. The final twelve verses of current versions of this gospel - about sightings of the 'risen' Master, his instruction to the disciples to 'go to every part of the world and proclaim the gospel' and a warning that those who do not believe will be 'condemned'[39] - were written by a different author and added years later. Scholars believe the extra passages were added to bring 'Mark' into line with the Second and Third Gospels.

In the First Gospel, Yeshua is primarily a great humanitarian who impresses people with his character and accomplishments. He performs miracles to help the unfortunate and downtrodden, not as 'signs' that he is divinely ordained (that came later, in the Fourth Gospel). It's light on dialogue, heavy on miracles, and he drives out a lot of demons. 'Mark's' Yeshua was the Messiah, but the Messiah in secret until his final week. The disciples are constantly urged not to tell anyone who he is or what he has done.

Everything that appears in 'Mark' also appears 'Matthew', 'Luke' or both, but there is hardly any consensus with 'John'.

---

[38]   There's no mention of these in Paul's letters either.

[39]   Post script to 'Mark', 'Mark' 16:15

Being the first to be written, it is tempting to think of 'Mark' as closer to the facts than the other gospels. This may be true, but the author was no dispassionate historian. He was a creative writer and theologian applying his own agenda to the stories he had heard to convince his readers of his point of view.

35. The Second Gospel, 'Matthew', goes out of its way to integrate Yeshua's life with the Hebrew Scriptures

The Second Gospel, 'Matthew', was written between 80-90 CE, probably for a Jewish-Christian community in Syria. Although named after one of Yeshua's twelve disciples, the actual writer is unknown. He was clearly well versed in Jewish scripture and customs and eager to present Yeshua as the fulfilment of certain prophecies in the Hebrew Scriptures. According to him, Yeshua was the Messiah destined to suffer at the hands of the gentiles to atone for the sins of the Jewish nation. Whenever you see a phrase like 'This took place to fulfil what had been spoken through the prophets'[40] or 'it is written.....' you're reading a passage from 'Matthew'. Hence the Second is the most Jewish of the gospels.

'Matthew' copied out long chunks of the First Gospel but gave them a more Jewish slant. Perhaps he thought that 'Mark' had not emphasised this enough and wanted to address the balance. He clearly believed that the new movement was for Jews, affirming the authority of the Torah[41]. He spared no derision for Jews who did not accept Yeshua as the Messiah, and was largely responsible for the idea they, not the Romans, were responsible for his death, a theme later reinforced in the Fourth Gospel.

---

[40]   Matthew 12:17
[41]   Matthew 5:17-19

Among the highlights of the Second Gospel is the Sermon on the Mount[42], one of the most beautiful and persuasive passages ever written. (The Third Gospel also has a version, but it is different.) However, no unbiased scholars believe that it was delivered as a single speech. It is more likely to be a collection of teachings that had been shared with many audiences at different times. And it couldn't have been delivered from a 'mountain'. There are no mountains in Galilee!

36. The Second Gospel endorses the doctrine of the Holy Trinity and the papacy

Experts detect more than one writer at work in the finished script of the Second Gospel. For instance, in Chapter Ten Yeshua tells his inner circle, 'Go nowhere amongst the gentiles, and enter no town of the Samaritans, but go rather to the lost sheep of the house of Israel.'[43] This is the authentic voice of the original author.

In the closing verses, the risen Master instructs his disciples to 'Go .. and make disciples of all nations, baptising them in the name of the Father and of the Son and of the Holy Spirit, and teaching them to observe all that I have commanded you.'[44] Thus in a few words a later writer/editor sanctioned global evangelism and the doctrine of the Holy Trinity, and a further passage[45] appears to justify the papacy. The Roman authorities at work? What do you think?

---

[42] Matthew Ch 5, 6 and 7
[43] Matthew 10:5-7
[44] Matthew 28: 19-20
[45] Matthew 16:18

37. The Third Gospel is the most pro-gentile

The Third Gospel was written between 80-90 CE. It is named after Luke, 'the beloved physician' mentioned in one of Paul's letters[46], but it was not written by him. Like the other gospels, the name was assigned later. Those who argue that this Luke was indeed the author point to several passages in Acts where he refers to Paul's missionary group as 'we', but most scholars are not convinced. The same author also wrote Acts of the Apostles.

The author was highly literate and keen to make Christianity respectable among educated Greek and Roman citizens in the gentile world. Whereas 'Matthew' portrayed Yeshua as the prophesised Hebrew Messiah sent to rescue the Jews, 'Luke' portrayed him as the saviour of all humankind, his Jewish origins less important.

Although written around the same time as the Second Gospel, the Third differs in many important details. For example, this birth story features the heavily pregnant Maryām (the Aramaic for Mary) riding a donkey eighty miles from Nazareth to Bethlehem and shepherds but no wise men[47]. Also it alone claims that Yeshua and John the Baptist were cousins. It has fewer miracles and more parables, and its Sermon on the Mount is much shorter and delivered from a 'level place'.

When you read the gospels in parallel, you can't help noticing that 'Luke' repeatedly takes a story from the other Synoptic Gospels and exaggerates it, often making a plausible account unbelievable. For example, all the gospels report that Yeshua rebuked the person who cut off a guard's ear at the time of his arrest in the Garden

---

[46]   Colossians 4:14

[47]   I'll have more to say about discrepancies in the birth stories later.

of Gethsemene,[48] but in 'Luke' he went one further – he touched the ear and healed it[49].

Not everything in the First Gospel is included in the Third. It seems some passages were excluded because they did not support the author's gentile-friendly agenda.

38. By the end of the 1st Century CE, beliefs about Yeshua had changed

By the turn of the 1st and 2nd Centuries when the Fourth Gospel was written, life was very different from the days when Yeshua walked the Earth. Stories about him had been told and retold many times, and there is much evidence that the 'Chinese whispers' effect occurred[50]. Followers increasingly spoke of him as having god-like powers. In the Synoptics, Yeshua is *like* G_d; in the Fourth Gospel, he *is* G_d. He had become the 'Christ', nothing like the real Yeshua at all!

By the 10th decade there seemed little hope of divine rescue for the Jews, and the Christians needed reassurance that their saviour would return. The gospel writers had to reinforce belief, strengthen resolve and generate optimism in the face of hostility, ridicule and persecution.

---

[48] Mark 14:47, Matt 26:51-52 and John 18:10-11

[49] Luke 22:50-51

[50] The Chinese Whispers effect happens when a story gets exaggerated through repeated telling. Errors typically accumulate in the retellings. Reasons for changes include erroneous corrections and deliberate alterations.

39. Until Biblical scholarship took off in the 19ᵗʰ Century, the Fourth Gospel was thought to be the most factual

Before the 19ᵗʰ Century, the Fourth Gospel ('John') was thought to be the most factual, but this is no longer the case. Today, 'John's' Gospel is regarded more as an ingenious treatise using Yeshua as a vehicle to get the author's theological views across rather than as a work of fact. He uses miraculous signs and lengthy discourses to get his point across.

Until recent times a peculiar kind of reverse logic had been applied; since the Bible is the word of G_d, it was argued, the discourses must be accurate, therefore the author must have been there to hear them!

40. There are three authors named 'John' in the New Testament

Five New Testament books bear the name 'John' – the gospel, three letters and Revelation. Despite the mountain of evidence, church dignitaries continue to insist that these were all written by Yeshua's disciple John, but this cannot be so. Expert analysis of the texts shows that there were probably three Johns: the first wrote the gospel and the first letter; a second wrote the second and third letters; a third 'John' wrote Revelation. John the disciple would have had to be well into his nineties at the time the Fourth Gospel was written. Although it is believed he enjoyed great longevity, the gospel would have been an exceptional achievement for such an elderly man!

Moreover, Yeshua's predictions of the imminent coming of the Kingdom had proved false, so these teachings were toned down. Also, by the '90s Christianity had separated from Judaism, and not very amicably. Jews who accepted Yeshua as the Messiah were expelled from synagogues and churches accepted members who had not previously converted to Judaism. The author of the Fourth Gospel made certain that Jews – not Romans - were blamed for murdering the Son of G_d.

Moreover, 'John's' Gospel has no mention of the 'Transfiguration' – an incident in which Yeshua was said to have taken three disciples, Cephas, Tiago and John, up a high mountain[51], met with the ghosts of the ancient prophets Moses and Elijah, and become dazzling white.[52] A voice rang out from a cloud, 'This is my Son, the beloved; listen to him,' echoing the words allegedly spoken at Yeshua's baptism. The disciples fell to the ground, terrified; he touched them and told them not to be afraid. When they eventually looked up, Elijah and Moses had gone and the four were alone. Yeshua told them not to tell anyone about what they had seen until after the Son of Man had risen from the dead.

The disciple John was one of the three who witnessed it, so why, if he wrote the Fourth Gospel, is there no mention of this extraordinary event? Surely a striking incident like this would have been worthy of a mention in all four gospels?

Perhaps we are not supposed to believe that it actually happened. Perhaps the authors intended it to allegorical, representative of the moment when three senior disciples came to believe that Yeshua was the Messiah. After all, when Dr Martin Luther King said he had been to the top of the mountain and seen the Promised Land, no-one thought he had actually climbed a mountain!

---

[51]   Remember, there are no high mountains in Galilee.

[52]   Mark 9:2-8, also Matthew 17:1-8 and Luke 9:28-36

41. All four gospels show Jews in a bad light

All four gospels show Jews in a bad light, but the Fourth is the most derisive. Throughout this gospel, 'the Jews' are lumped together as a group, and the term used disparagingly. For example:

> '*The Jews* replied, 'We are not permitted to put anyone to death'.'[53]

> 'Joseph of Arimathea, who was a disciple of Jesus although a secret one because of fear of *the Jews*.....'[54]

> '*The Jews* had already agreed that anyone who confessed Jesus to be the Messiah would be put out of the synagogue.' [55]

42. The Fourth Gospel is completely different from the Synoptics

The Fourth Gospel has little in common with the other three gospels in style or substance. Whereas the Synoptics were largely attempts to *describe* Yeshua's ministry, 'John's' primary aim was to *explain* its meaning. It is notable for the numerous lengthy speeches given by the Christ character.

For example, Chapter Four details a lengthy conversation between Yeshua and a Samaritan woman by a well in which he impresses her with his clairvoyant abilities (he seemed to know the details of her marital history) and wisdom. Actually it's more of a sermon than a conversation, centred on the person of Yeshua as the Christ,

---

[53]   John 18:31
[54]   John 19:38
[55]   John 9:22

who he was and why he came to Earth, in rich metaphorical language. 'Everyone who drinks of this water will be thirsty again,' he tells her, 'but those who drink of the water that I will give them will never be thirsty.' [56]

The question is, how exactly could these words have reached the gospel writer? It's unlikely that Yeshua or the woman wrote them down, and neither could the disciples because the narrative says they weren't there. Although the author says they appeared soon after the incident, Yeshua would have had to recall and dictate his words to them. And all this assumes they could write and had writing materials conveniently to hand.

Very few Bible experts believe that Yeshua actually delivered the lengthy speeches attributed to him in the Fourth Gospel. Indeed, according to author and professor Dr Marcus Borg, two hundred top biblical scholars meeting as long ago as 1933 were only able to accept 20% of the sayings attributed to Yeshua in the gospels as genuine – and none, yes none, of the Fourth Gospel discourses. They were put into Yeshua's mouth to express the author's theological views. They are words that Yeshua never said and *would never have said*.

43. The four gospels cannot be combined into one coherent narrative

Some writers of yesteryear attempted to combine the four gospels into one coherent narrative, as if they truthfully describe the same events from slightly different perspectives. They do not; there are too many contradictions. For a start, most of the material in the Fourth Gospel is not found in the other gospels, and most of the material in the other gospels is not found in the Fourth. From

---

[56]   John 4:7-26

the opening passages about the pre-existence of the Word, the contrast could not be greater. Yeshua, the reluctant Messiah of the Synoptics who taught the coming of the Kingdom of G_d, has been replaced in the Fourth Gospel with an other-worldly 'Christ' making extravagant claims about his own identity. And that isn't the only difference.

In the Synoptics, Yeshua ministered in Galilee for less than a year before heading south to Jerusalem to confront the authorities. In the Fourth Gospel, his ministry lasted 3-4 years and Galilee is barely mentioned. The sequence of events is also different. For instance, the well-known incident in which an angry Yeshua drives the moneychangers from the Jerusalem temple takes place in the second chapter of 'John', but in his final week in the Synoptics. There is no birth story in the Fourth Gospel, and no mention of Bethlehem; Yeshua is explicitly described as coming from Nazareth. Nor does it say what happened to the risen Yeshua after he had appeared to the disciples.

Adding the gospels together and pretending the result makes sense is like adding apples and oranges and calling them bananas!

44. 'I am the way, the truth, and the life'

In the Fourth Gospel, Yeshua repeatedly refers to himself as the Son of G_d[57] and claims that 'No-one come to the Father except by me.'[58] In the Synoptics he makes no such claims until pressed by the authorities in the trial narratives. In the Fourth Gospel Yeshua talks at length about himself: 'I am' he says, 'the bread of life'[59],

---

[57] 'For God so loved the world that he gave his only son, that everyone who believes in him may not perish but may have eternal life.' (John 3:16)

[58] John 14:6

[59] John 6:35, 48 and 51

'the light of the world'[60], 'the good shepherd'[61], 'the resurrection and the life'[62], 'the true vine'[63] and 'the way, the truth, and the life'[64]. 'He who has seen me has seen the Father',[65] says he. But in the Synoptics he says no such things, even rebuking a man who calls him 'Good Teacher.' 'Why do you call me good?' he replies. 'No-one is good except G_d alone'.[66] He insists that he is not to be worshipped: 'Worship the Lord your G_d and serve only him[67],' he says.

In the Synoptics, Yeshua is a human being, enjoying his food, quarrelling with his family, losing his temper, exasperated with the disciples, and sweating blood as his execution approaches. But in the Fourth Gospel he is no longer one of them. He tells his disciples, 'You are from below, I am from above; you are of this world, I am not of this world.'[68]

45. There are fewer miracles in 'John', but they are more dramatic

The Fourth Gospel has far fewer miracles — only four - but they are the most dramatic: turning water into wine[69], walking on the sea[70], healing a blind man[71] and bringing the stinking corpse of

---

[60]   John 8:12 and 9:5
[61]   John 10:11
[62]   John 11:25
[63]   John 15:1
[64]   John 14:6
[65]   John 14:9
[66]   Luke 18:19
[67]   Matthew 4:10
[68]   John 8:23
[69]   John 2:1-11
[70]   John 6:16-21
[71]   John 9:1-41

Lazarus back to life.[72] Neither Lazarus nor this particular blind man appear in the other gospels, nor does turn water into wine. Moreover, in the Synoptics, the disciples are sworn to silence when Yeshua performs a miracle; in the Fourth Gospel miracles are performed as 'signs' to demonstrate who he was. This is especially true in the case Yeshua's miraculous healings. In 'Mark' they were expressions of G_d's presence and power; in 'John' they were proof who the author believed Yeshua was – the Son of G_d no less.

It is obvious from the character of the gospel accounts – Acts and the New Testament letters too – that each writer added such details and chose such expressions as suited his own individual purpose, taking hearsay as the main basis of their stories.

46. The gospels are not objective descriptions

Should we be concerned that the gospels differ from each other in important respects? After all, no-one would expect four separate accounts of anything to match exactly, as any policeman or lawyer would affirm. But these are not unbiased descriptions; indeed, they are not factual descriptions at all. Small details of time and place, actions and dialogue did not appear to over concern the authors. For example, it seems that none of them ever visited Galilee since they were unfamiliar with its landscape.

Those who believe that the gospels are of divine origin have some explaining to do, for there are too many inconsistencies both *within* them and *between* them for them to be the infallible word of G_d. Surely G_d surely does not get the facts wrong or contradict itself? The gospels do!

---

[72] John 11:1-44

47. The gospels give incomplete accounts of Yeshua's life

The gospels are *not* complete. They cover only a handful of years, completely omitting Yeshua's teens and twenties. We know nothing of his education, how he became to be radicalised, how his thinking developed as he matured, nor why he chose to take on the mantle of John the Baptist after the latter's arrest. Nor, we must assume, are they complete statements of his teachings.

We have no way of knowing whether he would have approved of the gospels or the ideas in the New Testament letters. His disciples showed precious little understanding during his lifetime and he often had to take them aside and explain what he meant. How much harder would it have been to get it right decades later?

48. The gospels give the impression of historical accuracy because they combine real events with fictionalised events

The gospels give the impression of historical accuracy because they combine real events and real people with fictional events and fictionalised events only loosely based on fact. For instance, there really was a King Herod, a Chief Priest named Caiaphas, a Roman Prefect named Pontius Pilate and a woman named Mary Magdalene. We can't be sure they all behaved as described, though; for example, there are grave doubts about the gospel accounts of Pilate's role in Yeshua's crucifixion, as we shall see. This is not surprising since the gospel accounts rely mostly on hearsay. Hearsay would not be accepted as evidence in a modern court of law, and nor would a wise person rely on it for accurate information about another person.

The authors were not there at the time, never met Yeshua nor anyone who had met him. And they were hardly impartial!

49. Few people take the trouble to read the gospels in parallel and in detail

Why are so few practising Christians aware that the gospels are very different? Take the post-resurrection appearances and ascension stories for instance – the four are completely at odds with each other! So are the accounts of Yeshua's nativity, trial, execution and burial. These are surely the most important passages in the Christian scriptures! The problem is, few people take the trouble to read the gospel accounts side by side in detail. Only when we compare them do we realise that the authors' accounts of *the same event* are often so different as to be incompatible. If you want to investigate further, read the gospel accounts of how Yeshua recruited his disciples. All quite different!

You could argue, as many have, that if you asked four eyewitnesses to describe any event you would have four different versions. It's why it is often so hard to disentangle the truth in court hearings. *But these authors were not eyewitnesses* and *three of them were not independent,* since we know 'Matthew' and 'Luke' used 'Mark' as their main source. The only logical conclusion is that the gospels are *not* an accurate record of events in the order in which they occurred, and neither is Acts. Probably the authors, relying on word of mouth, didn't know the facts, and they made full use of artistic licence to maintain their literary flow.

50. There are several possible reasons why the gospels repeatedly disagree

There are many possible reasons why the gospels frequently disagree with each other; you may be able to think of a few of your own. They include:

- The stories passed down orally to each of them and the details of each story were different.
- They each researched the stories and uncovered different facts.
- They selected those parts of the story which appealed to them, such as 'Matthew' preferring the Wise Men in the nativity stories and 'Luke' the shepherds.
- None of them had all the facts, being separated from the events by time, language and distance.
- They were more concerned with making theological points than getting the details right.
- Each gospel author had a different agenda, chose only those facts which fit, and used artistic licence to create the rest. In other words, they made some of it up!

Perhaps it's all of the above! The gospel contradictions resonate like the work of a group of individuals creating an alibi for each other but failing to check that their stories tally. Many years ago a journalist shared with me the guiding principle of his profession: 'Never let the facts get in the way of a good story.' It seems the gospel authors were better journalists than historians! The evidence is right there in the pages of the New Testament itself.

ACTS OF THE APOSTLES

51. Acts has almost nothing to say about the life and teachings of Yeshua

Acts of the Apostles was written by the same man who wrote the Third Gospel. Its main purpose was to describe the events that unfolded after the crucifixion, so it has almost nothing to say about the life and teachings of Yeshua. It starts with the disciples gathering to decide what to do after the reappearance of their Master, tells how Christianity began to take shape and spread across the Eastern Mediterranean in the second third of the 1st Century and how it began to separate itself from Judaism. It ends with the Apostle Paul in captivity in Rome awaiting execution.

The first major event in Acts is the Ascension: Yeshua, now the Christ figure, is lifted up and taken away (presumably to heaven) on a cloud[73]. This immediately raises one of those contradictions for which the New Testament ought to be better known: at the end of 'Luke's' Gospel[74] the Christ figure is carried up to heaven on the day of his resurrection: in Acts the Christ figure appears to the disciples (now renamed apostles) *over a forty day period* before a cloud whisks him away.[75] Remember, these accounts were written by the same author: either he had a poor memory, or there is some artistic licence here!

---

[73] Acts 1:9-10
[74] Luke 24:13-50
[75] Acts 1:3

Pentecost – a festival in which Jews from many nations gathered in Jerusalem – follows soon after. According to Acts[76], the apostles were together one morning when they heard the sound of a violent wind, tongues of fire appeared, and they were filled with the 'Holy Spirit'. These simple Galileans immediately started addressing the crowd in their own languages. The Apostle Cephas delivered a lengthy sermon[77], winning over many converts, and soon after discovered he had acquired the power to heal. Acts says he cured a man lame from birth who leapt for joy around the temple[78].

In the years that followed, the apostles travelled widely, preaching and attracting converts. Some accomplished great works and some were executed. But most of Acts, about two-thirds, is devoted to the activities of one man, the Apostle Paul of Tarsus. He, not Yeshua, was the real founder of Christianity.

52. We can compare Act's version of events with the versions that appear in Paul's letters

One of the most interesting things about Acts is that it offers us the opportunity to compare its description of events with the versions that appear in Paul's letters. We find that the Acts account is embellished in every case where an incident appears in both documents. For example, Acts' account of Paul's vision on the road to Damascus is far more dramatic than Paul's own. In his letter to the Galatians, Paul stated that he had a revelation. 'God..... was pleased to reveal his son to me,' he wrote, 'so that I might proclaim him among the gentiles.'[79]

---

[76]   Acts 2:1–47

[77]   Acts 2:14–26

[78]   Acts 3:1–10

[79]   Galatians, 1:13–16

Acts, written thirty years later, is much more dramatic:[80] Paul (previously known as Saul) saw a 'blinding light' and heard a voice saying, 'Saul, why do you persecute me?' He asked, 'Who are you?' The voice replied, 'I am Yeshua, who you are persecuting.' Saul was struck blind, although he later miraculously regained his sight. He changed his name to Paul, and instead of arresting Yeshua's followers took it upon himself to become their leader. Paul referred to this incident in several of his letters, but he never mentioned a blinding light, loss of sight or a heavenly voice.

---

[80] Acts 9:1-20

53. Hebrews was written before 70 CE

Hebrews was written by an unknown author. It was once thought to have been written by Paul of Tarsus, but this has long since been refuted. It is one of the earliest New Testament texts. We know it was written before 70 CE because it refers to temple sacrifices, which ceased when the temple was destroyed that year.

In the years following the crucifixion, very few people believed in Yeshua as G_d's messenger, the Messiah or G_d's son[81]. Christians were figures of fun, cruelly persecuted and openly mocked. They needed all the comfort and encouragement they could get.

It seems to have been written to a group of Jewish Christians in Jerusalem who were feeling discouraged because their saviour had not yet returned. Its words on faith are inspirational:

> 'Now faith is the assurance of things hoped for, the conviction of things not seen. By faith we understand that the worlds were prepared by the word of G_d, so that what is seen was made from things that are not visible.'[82]

Nowadays it is not only philosophers but scientists too who tell us that everything we see has its origins in an invisible world of

---

[81]   'Mark's' explanation was that Yeshua himself restricted the spread of the news, but this is not tenable because the same author also says he was mobbed by crowds.

[82]   Hebrews 11:1-3

energy and information. Does it stretch the imagination too far to suppose that this is what the author meant by the 'word of G_d'?

54. Although they bear the names of apostles, the later letters couldn't have been written by them

The final documents of the New Testament are the letters of 'James', 'Jude', 'Peter' (1 and 2), 'John' (1, 2 and 3) and the Revelation to John. They expand on the teachings of the early church at a time when Christians faced persecution and were struggling to explain why Yeshua had failed to reappear to establish the promised Kingdom of G_d.

Although they bear the names of the Apostles Cephas and John and Yeshua's brothers Tiago and Jude (Judas), they couldn't have been written by them. They reached their final form late in the 1st Century and, in the case of 'Peter's' second letter, around 125 CE. Tiago is known to have been executed by stoning around 62 CE, and the others were almost certainly dead by then. As was the practice in those days, the authors used the names of the apostles to add authority to their own ideas.

The letter of 'James' challenges Paul's assertion that salvation is by faith alone. It argues that faith is demonstrated by good works and gives practical tips for living the Christian life.[83]

'Jude's' letter is the shortest, written in the name of the 'brother of Tiago,' and by implication the brother of Yeshua. The name may have been shortened from Judas to Jude to avoid confusion with the traitorous Mr Iscariot. The letter denounces the 'false

---

[83] James 2:14-18

teachings' of scoffers, people 'devoid of Spirit' who are causing divisions[84] – presumably unconvinced Jews or the early Gnostics.

Two letters are named after the apostle Cephas. The first dates from the end of the 1st Century. It assures Christians that suffering for the sake of their Lord is noble and worthy. The second was the last biblical text to be written, around 125 CE, warning the faithful not to listen to false teachers and excusing the uncomfortable fact that the Kingdom promised by Yeshua nearly a century earlier had still not materialised. Both were written in fluent Greek, but they are so different in style and content that they are very unlikely to have been the work of the same man. Neither is afforded much significance by the modern church.

All three letters titled 'John' date from around the turn of the 1st Century, yet one is of a very different style to the others. The first declares that Yeshua was a real man who had lived not just in spirit, but in a body. The second warns of false teachers, and the third praises the virtue of humility. Scholars attribute these letters, the Fourth Gospel and Revelation to at least three different authors, not necessarily named 'John'.

55. Revelation was never intended as a prediction of what will happen at the end of time

The New Testament closes with the nightmarish book of Revelation, a vision of cosmic struggles with G_d emerging triumphant, his enemies vanquished. It was written around 90-95 CE on the Island of Patmos, a penal colony, by a man known as 'John the Revelator'. It symbolises the suffering of Christians at the hands of Nero, the Roman Emperor from 54 to 68 CE. The

---

[84]   Jude 17-19

text is rich in symbolism used to camouflage his meaning from the Roman persecutors.

Revelation was intended to offer hope. It predicted the imminent appearance of a saviour who would destroy their conquerors, rebuild Jerusalem and restore their independence. What Revelation is not, nor was ever intended to be, is a prediction of what will happen to humanity at the end of time. It is a book of its own time and place; indeed, when the contents of the New Testament were finalised towards the end of the 4th Century, its inclusion was hotly disputed.

The Revelator would doubtless be astonished to discover that scholars were still grappling with it 1,900 years later! No doubt Paul and the others would feel the same about their letters!

56. The purpose of the New Testament writings was to instruct the faithful and reinforce belief

The New Testament is a record of the thoughts of a few[85] G_d seeking, mainly Jewish, men, representing a community of several thousand people who lived around the Eastern Mediterranean long ago. Their purpose was to instruct the faithful and reinforce belief. They fervently believed that Yeshua was sent by G_d and wanted their readers to be as convinced as they. They recorded their *impressions* of events which they had heard about and which, to them, were highly significant.

They didn't have all the facts at their disposal, nor did they know what we know now, for instance that the world is a globe, how big

---

[85] Not counting the tens of thousands of writers, editors, copyists and translators who took the original manuscripts and altered them down the centuries, a process which still continues today.

it is, what is above the clouds or below the ground, or how babies are conceived. They were simply telling their readers how they felt about their Master using stories and sayings as their vehicle. There are plenty of reasons why we must not treat the New Testament as a work of historical fact. If we do we miss the point. It's a great read, but the meaning is not to be found by taking it literally but reading between the lines, and perhaps that's what the authors intended. You must get behind the language used; words like 'Lord', 'salvation', 'sin', 'heaven', 'righteous', 'mercy' and 'God' are steeped in the symbolism and imagery of the first few centuries and the Middle Ages.[86]

When read in the right way, we find wisdom and insights which can guide us through life and help us find greater fulfilment and happiness. Bishop John Shelby Spong describes the gospels as 'beautiful portraits painted by 1st Century Jewish artists, designed to point the reader towards that which is, in fact, accurate and real.'[87] As Buddhists say, they are like a finger pointing to the moon, but they are not, in fact, the moon.

---

[86] Prof Marcus Borg's excellent *Speaking Christian* gives many examples of how the ancient Greek language has been inadequately translated and some important meanings distorted.

[87] In his ground-breaking book, *Why Christianity Must Change Or Die*

WHAT WE KNOW ABOUT YESHUA

57. We know next to nothing about Yeshua

Most religions can be traced back to a wise, knowledgeable and spiritually aware teacher, usually with great charisma, who claims to have answers to the deeper questions. Often they claim that G-d spoke directly to them. Yeshua certainly held this appeal for his close followers and continues to do so for millions around the world. But the truth is, we know next to nothing about him! We know a great deal about the main historical figures of that era – Nero, Julius Caesar, Cleopatra, Marcus Aurelius and so on. We know more about characters that pre-date Yeshua by several hundred years, such as Socrates, Plato and Alexander the Great. We also know more about other New Testament figures such as Pontius Pilate, Caiaphas and Paul of Tarsus than the main man.

The dilemma faced by anyone interested in the *real* Yeshua is this: there are no independent sources, and the real person cannot be found in the gospels because they present a highly selective and distorted view. Josephus and the other historical authors described Yeshua as an exceptional man who suffered the usual fate of dissenters in Roman Palestine, but the New Testament authors had someone quite different in mind – *the person Yeshua had become for them during the time that had elapsed since his execution decades earlier.* He had become the mystical Christ figure described in the writings of Paul in the 50s and brought to life in the ingenious narrative that is the Fourth Gospel in the 90s, a god-man who was so virtuous he was incapable of sin, a miracle worker who had power over life and death, and who offered up his life knowing he was destined to be the saviour of humankind.

58. We don't even know what he looked like

The popular image of Yeshua pictured in innumerable paintings and etchings is actually a misrepresentation. Yeshua would have resembled any other rural Galilean Jewish male of that era. The tall, long brown-haired, pale faced man depicted in European portraiture wearing a long, flowing robe, cannot possibly resemble his real appearance. Remains of poor Jewish men from that time reveal that they were short by today's standards, thick set, dark-skinned, bearded and with dark tousled hair[88]. Whether he was fat, thin, long-haired, short-haired, healthy, fit – we will never know for sure. Nor will we ever know what he sounded like. Did he have a deep voice or a high-pitched, squeaky voice? We don't know. The only adjective describing his speech in the gospels is 'authoritative'.

59. The gospel authors had no dependable way of checking their facts

Nowadays if you wanted to write a biography of someone who died half a century ago, like Dr Martin Luther King, Sir Winston Churchill or President Kennedy for instance, you would search the internet, visit a library and bookstore and look for film clips and

---

[88] A BBC documentary series called 'Son of God' made in 2001 featured a recreation of the head and face of a typical 1st Century Jew.

old newsreels. You could even try to make contact with people who knew him, although they would either be in their dotage, their memories faded, or very young at the time in question. But bear in mind, the average seventy year-old today is much fitter and more mentally alert than they were in the 1st Century. The life expectancy of an average Galilean in Yeshua's time was probably no more than thirty-two years.

Now imagine it's the year 80 CE, fifty years since Yeshua's painful death. You're writing a biography of him. You live in Syria, Turkey or Rome, hundreds of miles from Palestine. You've never visited Galilee or Jerusalem and know little about the area. You have never lived as a Jew in a predominantly Jewish region, so are not as fully steeped in Jewish culture as was Yeshua and his disciples. You don't speak his native language, Aramaic. All his family and close companions (except perhaps one elderly disciple, who is blind) are dead and they don't speak your language, Greek. You try to piece together his teachings, but have no recordings of his actual words, intonations and gestures. His followers show you a hand written copy of an earlier parchment ('Mark') and share anecdotes with you, based on what they've heard, but you have no reliable way of checking whether their version of events is correct.

Today we know exactly what Dr Martin Luther King said at the Washington Monument in 1963 or President Kennedy at the Berlin Wall that same year. We can even go back further, for instance we have recordings of Winston Churchill's wartime speeches in the 1940s and his warnings about the Soviet threat in the 1950s. Their content is beyond dispute. But we can never know, for instance, what was said during Yeshua's trial or the Sermon on the Mount[89].

---

[89]   If they ever took place, which is disputed (as we'll see).

Now jump forward to the present day. You obtain a partial biography of Yeshua written more than nineteen centuries ago – it's called a gospel. It's been copied, miscopied, edited, added to and translated many times. It's been amended many times by people with vested interests to ensure it's 'on message'. How reliable is it as a factual account? And yet a third of the people in the world live under political and religious systems based on these writings!

60. We can place Yeshua in a specific historical, geographical and cultural setting

Even though we can't trust the gospels as accurate accounts, they contain clues which place Yeshua in a specific historical, geographical and cultural setting. These clues can be cross-referenced by historians, linguists and archaeologists against other sources. But that doesn't mean that everything written about him in the gospels is true, or that everything that mattered about him was recorded.

To reveal the real man, we have to indulge in detective-style deduction. So what *do* we know?

61. Yeshua was a 1st Century Galilean Jew

Yeshua's Jewishness is one of the most important facts about him. He was born, lived and died a Jew, deeply rooted in his Jewish heritage. He answered to the title 'Rabbi'. He preached his own understanding of the Jewish scriptures. His moral teachings were largely based on them and not a word in the gospels suggests that he wanted to supplant them, only apply them more humanely.

That Yeshua was a Jew (not a Christian since there was no such thing in his day) cannot be emphasised enough.

62. Yeshua was a healer who attracted large crowds, told stories and was put to death for sedition

As we've seen, the handful of contemporary historical sources that exist describe Yeshua as a healer from Galilee who attracted large crowds, told stories and was put to death because he refused to pay taxes to the Romans. But did this make him unique? Not entirely. There were a large number of extraordinary healers and holy men in Palestine at that time, mainly considered harmless by the ruling authorities. But for some reason this Nazarene's memory lived on. Indeed, he made such an impression on certain people that they continued to tell stories about him long after his death.

He must have been a remarkable healer and exorcist, so much so that the Jewish leaders called him a 'sorcerer'. The gospels say that what made him stand out was his practice of telling the healed that their sins were forgiven, which was a direct challenge to the authority of the priests. But this was not his only purpose. When sick people were healed, it made them acceptable again under the Purity Laws; they could then re-join society and participate in religious activities.

63. Yeshua was a human being

As a human, he had to eat, sleep, wash himself and (while the thought is distasteful to some Christians) go to the toilet like the rest of us. He could demonstrate all the human emotions including anger and fear. He could be loving, compassionate and tender, and he could also be desperate, frustrated, tearful and afraid. He could also be impatient, even with his own disciples.

64. As a boy, Yeshua was probably quite ordinary

As a boy, Yeshua was obviously intelligent but otherwise quite ordinary; certainly the villagers of Nazareth noticed nothing unique about him and, according to the gospels, were amazed when he started preaching. The family probably lived hand to mouth like most of their neighbours. Yeshua's father, Yehosef (Joseph), was the village carpenter; as a skilled man he must have been better off than most. After the birth stories, nothing more is said about him in the gospels, apart from an incident in Jerusalem when Yeshua was twelve. It is usually assumed that Yeshua joined the family carpentry business. Yehosef probably died before Yeshua began his public ministry, but his mother Maryām is mentioned several times in the gospels and in Acts.

Yeshua was not an only child: he had brothers and sisters. The First Gospel gives the names of his brothers – Tiago, Jose, Judas and Simon. Tiago (later known as James) became an important Christian leader in Jerusalem after his death.

Later reports of his teaching suggest that he had a thorough grounding in the Jewish scriptures, but any young Jewish boy could have had the same.

Nothing of Yeshua's childhood, adolescence and young manhood appears in the gospels between his birth and baptism other than a brief incident in the Third Gospel. We are told that when he was twelve years old his parents took him to Jerusalem to celebrate the Passover. Unbeknown to the author this would have been quite a trek through hostile territory[90]. After the festival his parents set out for home and had travelled a full day before they noticed their son was not with their party. They returned to Jerusalem and

---

[90] Between Nazareth and Jerusalem lay Samaria. Jews and Samaritans didn't get on.

found him debating with the temple teachers who were amazed at his knowledge and wisdom.[91] We have no way of knowing whether this incident really took place or was another example of 'Luke's' fertile imagination, but wonder how any parent could be so careless! And where were Yeshua's brothers and sisters at the time?

65. He was a rural dweller

Yeshua was a rural dweller. He moved among the small towns and villages of his native province. The cities of Galilee – Sepphoris, the capital, Tiberias and Scythopolis - do not feature in the gospel stories, but this does not mean he never went there. More likely the gospel writers never visited Galilee and had a poor knowledge of the area.

The Jerusalem set were dismissive of him because they thought him a jumped up country bumpkin from a backward and impoverished province. Some of his fellow Galileans were just as dismissive of his home village. 'Can anything good come out of Nazareth?' said one.[92]

66. He loved life and enjoyed company

The gospels portray Yeshua as a man with a genuine love of life who lived simply and enjoyed all types of company, especially when food and drink were involved. He spent time with people from all sections of society, even those whom the Torah branded unclean, such as lepers, beggars and women of the street. Even so, he needed frequent periods of solitude. He used spiritual practices

---

[91]   Luke 2: 41-50
[92]   John 1:46

such as fasting, deep contemplation and prayer, sometimes all night long.

67. He was a skilled orator

Yeshua was a skilled orator. He was a master of language. His words were impactful and carried authority. He could be dramatic. The gospels are rich in memorable stories and sayings with powerful messages. He made his audiences think, but also puzzled them with confusing and contradictory remarks. His answers and quick-fire retorts often 'put his opponents to shame.'[93] He used examples that his audiences could relate to, and sometimes which stretched the imagination.

He often shocked his listeners by overstating to get his point across. This is not always obvious to us today since printed words on a page are dry, and there is no record of how his words were spoken. Tone of voice, facial expression, hand gestures and so on can completely change the meaning of a sentence. When he told a young man to go and sell everything he had and give the money to the poor[94], was he smiling or serious? Did he have a sense of humour? There's little evidence of it in the gospels.

68. Meek and mild? No, he was outspoken and confrontational

Yeshua was no pushover and no respecter of reputations. He was outspoken and confrontational. He divided opinion. Some thought him crazy. This was a man who taught nonviolence and non-resistance against brutal oppressors and said one should love one's enemies; a man who fearlessly called the religious leaders

---

[93] Luke 13:17
[94] Matthew 19:21

of his day hypocrites[95], blind guides[96] and a brood of vipers[97] to their faces. In return they insulted him – he was a 'glutton and a drunkard, and a friend of tax collectors and sinners'[98].

Gentle Jesus meek and mild? Hardly!

69. Some saw him as a leader who could lead an uprising against the Romans

He attracted a following large enough to worry the Jewish leaders and the Roman occupiers. Some of his followers saw him as a potential leader who could lead an uprising against the Romans, although it's hard to imagine him riding a warhorse or thrusting a sword into anyone.

70. There is no evidence that Yeshua intended to start a new religion

There is no evidence in the gospels or anywhere else in the New Testament that Yeshua intended to start a new religion because he wanted his people to be better Jews. Yeshua was a religious man who cared deeply about the Jerusalem Temple, although he had little respect for the religious hierarchy of his day. He felt the whole system was in urgent need of reform having been corrupted by the priesthood. Reform would come automatically when the Kingdom of G_d was established on Earth.

---

[95] Matthew 23:3
[96] Matthew 23:24
[97] Matthew 3:7
[98] Matthew 11:19

71. His was a 'back to basics' campaign

Yeshua's was a 'back to basics' campaign, back to traditional Judaism. He sought only to see it come to fruition in G_d's kingdom with the twelve tribes of Israel (as featured in the Hebrew Scriptures) restored.

He and his followers generally observed the Law. Infringements such as plucking ears of grain on the Sabbath were infrequent and relatively minor. Besides, if he had preached that people could break G_d's laws while claiming to represent G_d, there would have been uproar. However, he wanted the rules to be applied sensitively. For example, when challenged over his observance of the strict rules of the Sabbath he replied, 'The Sabbath was made for humankind, and not humankind for the Sabbath.'[99]

The Second Gospel, the most pro-Jewish of the four, made this perfectly clear. 'Do not think that I have come to abolish the law or the prophets: I have come not to destroy but to fulfil. For truly I tell you... not one letter, not one stroke of a letter, will pass from the law until all is accomplished.'[100] The First Gospel, too, has Yeshua reaffirming the temple, the priests, purity laws and obedience to the sacrificial laws.[101]

Sometimes he gave the Law a new twist that made it even stronger: 'You have heard that it was said, you shall love your neighbour and hate your enemy. But I say to you, love your enemies and pray for those that persecute you.'[102] 'You have heard it said... You shall not swear falsely, but carry out the vows you have made to

---

[99] Mark 2:27

[100] Matthew 5:17

[101] See Mark 1:40-45. The leper is urged to show himself to the priest and be declared clean in accordance with Jewish law.

[102] Matthew 5: 43-46

the Lord. But I say to you, do not swear at all...... Let your word be Yes, Yes or No, No.'[103]

72. Paul of Tarsus disagreed with Yeshua over Jewish Law

Remarkably, the man who is widely credited with bringing Christian doctrine together, Paul of Tarsus[104], was not in agreement with Yeshua over Jewish Law. He regarded it as redundant. The death and resurrection of the saviour was a sure sign for him that the Kingdom of G_d was on its way and the old Law could be consigned to history. We can safely assume that Yeshua himself knew nothing of this.

Within a few decades of Yeshua's death a heated debate among Christians ensued in which Paul's view of the Law prevailed. By the end of the 1st Century neither circumcision nor observing the food laws was considered necessary.

73. The gospels don't say Yeshua was married, and they don't say he wasn't

Was Yeshua ever married? We don't know. The gospels don't say he was, and they don't say he wasn't. It would have been very unusual for a Jewish man at that time to remain single. Boys married young and children were highly valued, but any suggestion that Yeshua ever married or had sex is quickly dismissed by the church. Paul of Tarsus saw marriage as a concession to human (by which he meant male) frailty, but grudgingly conceded it was better to marry than burn with lust. How, then, could the Church acknowledge that Yeshua was a married man?

---

[103]   Matthew 5:33-37
[104]   A former Pharisee, remember.

Dan Brown's dollar spinning novel the Da Vinci Code, published in 2003, stirred up a hornets nest by suggesting that Yeshua had offspring with Mary Magdelene, but the controversy soon blew over. Imagine, then, the enmity when a distinguished Professor of Christian History, Karen King, announced in 2012 that she had discovered an ancient text which made explicit reference to him having a wife! She claimed that researchers had identified the words 'Yeshua said to them, 'my wife'' on an ancient fragment of papyrus[105]. Professor King said it revealed the concerns of early Christians on family matters. She told a conference of respected historians, 'From the very beginning, Christians disagreed about whether it was better not to marry, but it was over a century after Yeshua's death before they began appealing to his marital status to support their positions.'

The balance of probabilities suggests that Yeshua was married at some time, probably before his ministry began. We don't know what happened to his wife, although we can be fairly certain that she was not Mary Magdalene!

74. 'Son of Man' is usually interpreted as Yeshua himself, although sometimes ambiguous

In the gospels, Yeshua often refers to the 'Son of Man'. It was a common term which signified humility. Usually it meant 'humanity' or 'people like us.'

Son of Man is usually interpreted as Yeshua himself, although many passages are ambiguous. He seemed to be claiming that

---

[105] Harvard Professor Karen King unveiled the 4th-Century Coptic script at a 2012 conference in Rome. She said it was a copy of a gospel probably written in the 2nd century. She acknowledged that it does not prove that Yeshua had a wife, only that some early Christians thought he did.

he, as Son of Man, would be instrumental in heralding the forthcoming Kingdom of G_d. But we can't be certain this is what he meant.

Incidentally, when the Romans used the term Son of G_d, they were referring to the Emperor. It would have been extremely dangerous to refer to anyone else by this title because it would have been seen as a direct challenge to the Emperor.

75. By the end of the 1ˢᵗ Century most Jews had not accepted Yeshua as the Messiah

By the time the Fourth Gospel was written, Christianity had separated completely from Judaism, most Jews had not accepted Yeshua as the Messiah and the promised Kingdom of G_d had not materialised.

The problem for Christians was that Yeshua was nothing like the Messiah envisaged in the Hebrew Scriptures. Jews were anticipating a great military leader who would lead them to freedom from Roman control and restore the Twelve Tribes of Israel. He would ride a war-horse, not a donkey, and his weapon would be a sword, not words. The Messiah would certainly not die a shameful death normally reserved for rebels and common criminals. If he died, it would be gloriously, leading his people in battle to a great victory.

According to the Synoptics, the common people wanted Yeshua to be king, but he didn't claim any title for himself and told the disciples not to speak of it[106]. But if he really was the Messiah, why would he want to keep it secret? To avoid trouble

---

[106]   Matthew 16:20. In contrast, the Fourth Gospel was in no doubt that Yeshua saw himself as the Messiah.

with the authorities perhaps? Avoid ridicule? Or maybe he was concerned to maintain a low profile and not raise expectations too high.

Only in his last week, the gospels say, did he acknowledge it in public with his entry into Jerusalem on a donkey. This was a deliberate re-enactment of a Hebrew Bible prophecy and would have been understood by Jews everywhere as a kingship claim. But there's no evidence outside the gospels that this remarkable event ever took place. If it did, it would undoubtedly have caused alarm among the Jewish leaders charged with keeping the peace and avoiding confrontation with the Romans.

76. Yeshua is a respected prophet in other religions

Christianity is not the only religion to have a view on Yeshua. He is an esteemed prophet in at least two other religions:

    i.   Most Jews are still awaiting their Messiah. They do not regard Yeshua as the Messiah, but as a heretic who broke away from the faith and dishonoured Jewish Law. Jews are aware that Christians persecuted them for much of the last 1900 years on the false pretext that Jews were responsible for the death of their Saviour. Even so, some Jews have a profound respect for his moral teachings.

   ii.   Buddhists generally regard Yeshua as a great and holy teacher, although some of his teachings do not sit well with Buddhism (such as his emphasis on G_d and the Kingdom). Also some Buddhist teachings (such as reincarnation) are at odds with Christian teachings.

  iii. In Islam, Yeshua was a prophet who was born of a virgin and performed miracles. He was not the Son of G_d, however, because G_d is not a person and cannot have a son. Nor would G_d have allowed its son to be crucified.

iv. Hindus recognise Yeshua as a holy man, the embodiment of the supreme G_d, as they do the leaders of other great religions. But they do not believe he was the one and only incarnation of G_d.

A DISCIPLE OF JOHN THE BAPTIST

77. Yeshua's baptism is probably the first historical incident in the gospels

Carefully reading between the lines in all four gospels, it is hard to escape the conclusion that Yeshua came to people's attention as a disciple of John the Baptist – perhaps his leading disciple. Yeshua's baptism by John is probably the first historically reliable incident in the gospels. If there had been no Baptist, Yeshua's life would have turned out very differently; perhaps there would have been no ministry, no arrest and no crucifixion. Perhaps we would never have heard of him at all!

78. Jews believed that G-d would send a Messiah to redeem them

Jews had believed for a thousand years that they had a special covenant with their G_d. If they obeyed G_d's commands, they would prosper and be protected against their enemies; if not, they would face retribution. The Hebrew Scriptures told of many times the Jews had turned their backs on G_d's wishes and been punished, only for a prophet to appear and lead them back to righteous ways. One, Isaiah, had explicitly promised that G-d would send a Messiah to redeem the Jewish people and lead them to freedom from their oppressors.

The Baptist never claimed to be the Messiah, but spoke of one who would follow who would be greater than he. All four gospels state that he immediately recognised Yeshua as the Messiah.

79. John the Baptist was more popular and more troublesome than Yeshua

According to the gospels, John the Baptist was a reclusive holy man, well-known for preaching that a new world order was about to be established. People had better repent (confess and renounce their sins) prior to the coming of the Lord[107]. He lived simply in the wilderness. He wore clothing of camel's hair with a leather belt around his waist and his meagre diet consisted of locusts and wild honey. He baptised people by submerging them in the River Jordan to signify cleansing and delivery from their sins.

He caused quite a stir in the region. The gospels give the impression that the whole of Palestine was gripped by the activities of Yeshua, but Josephus (who lived at the same time as the gospel writers) tells us that John was more popular and more troublesome to the authorities. Herod Antipas, the puppet king who ruled over Galilee, thought that John's preaching would lead to an uprising which would force the Romans to intervene so he had him arrested and executed. But he left Yeshua alone.

The gospels give a different reason for John's arrest. They say that Antipas had recently divorced his wife and replaced her with a younger woman, Herodius. John had angered Antipas by criticising his behaviour, so Herodius persuaded her new husband to have him beheaded. The truth is probably a combination of the two: John's reaction to the marriage was probably not the only reason for his arrest, just the last straw.

Incredibly, some Christians (including, apparently, Pope Emeritus Benedict XVI) believe that John's head was placed in a sack, buried in a dung heap and discovered four hundred years later.

---

[107]   Mark 1:4

It has since been lost and rediscovered a number of times and is considered a sacred relic by the Catholic Church. A head purporting to be that of the Baptist has recently been re-buried in the Vatican, but there's absolutely no proof that it is genuine. More likely, Antipas had the real head quickly disposed of along with the rest of his body.

80. 'This is my son, the beloved,' said a voice from the clouds

To strengthen their case that Yeshua was indeed the promised Messiah, the Synoptic Gospels say that a miraculous event occurred at his baptism: as he emerged from the water, the Holy Spirit descended like a dove and a heavenly voice was heard. In the First and Third Gospels, it tells Yeshua, 'You are my son, the beloved. With you I am well pleased.' In 'Matthew's' Gospel it addresses the onlookers: 'This is my son, the beloved, with whom I am well pleased.' The Fourth Gospel has no voice from heaven; instead, the Baptist himself endorses Yeshua, saying, 'I myself have seen and have testified that this is the Son of G_d.'[108] Interestingly, the earliest of the New Testament writings, Paul's letters, make no mention of John the Baptist at all.

In the 21st Century anyone who claimed to have heard such a voice would of course be admitted to a psychiatric establishment! But in 1st Century Palestine, it seems some people were quite prepared to believe in a voice from the clouds.

81. But still the Baptist was not convinced

Here's a curious thing. The Second and Third Gospels both say that after his arrest the Baptist sent a message to Yeshua from his

---

[108] John 1:31-35

prison cell.[109] Should we assume that Antipas's prison was like a modern open prison where the inmates can receive visitors and communicate easily with the outside world? Seems unlikely!

The message asked if Yeshua really was the Messiah or whether they should expect another. His response was effectively, 'Yes I am.' Referencing a passage in Isaiah[110], he replied: 'The blind receive their sight, the lame walk, the lepers are cleansed, the deaf hear, the dead are raised, and the poor have good news brought to them. And blessed is anyone who takes no offence at me.' This passage presents Yeshua as fulfilling the ancient prophecy; he was indeed the Messiah and the Kingdom was already on its way.

Don't you think this is odd? Two gospels say that the Baptist was not convinced that Yeshua was the Messiah despite a voice from heaven saying, 'You are my son, the Beloved'?' This would have persuaded most people! How could John have doubted it? And how did this inconsistency escape the authors?

82. Yeshua never abandoned his faith in his mentor

The evidence points to John the Baptist as Yeshua's mentor. If events had turned out differently, perhaps Yeshua would have played a bit part in history as the Baptists' best known, brightest and unluckiest disciple. But this would not have suited the gospel writers. They needed to explain why Yeshua sought baptism from a man they considered to be his spiritual inferior, or why the 'Son of G_d', needed remission of his sins. They also needed to convince their readers that Yeshua was who they said he was at a time when his prediction that the Kingdom of G_d would be established within a generation had failed to come true.

---

[109] Matthew 11: 2-6 and Luke 7:18-23. There is no mention of this in Mark.
[110] Isaiah 35:5-9

Yeshua was convinced that G-d had called him to carry on the work of the Baptist, to proclaim the coming of a new world order and urge the Jewish people to repent. He never abandoned his faith in his mentor. He repeatedly referred to him, and towards the end of his life told an audience of Chief Priests and Elders: 'The tax collectors and prostitutes are going to the Kingdom of G_d ahead of you, for John (the Baptist) came to you... and you did not believe him, but the tax collectors and the prostitutes believed him.'[111]

He echoed the Baptist's teachings but he did not try to emulate his lifestyle. Yeshua did not lead an austere life. He lived among people, enjoyed a good meal and a cup or two of wine. John stayed in one place and people sought him out; Yeshua moved around. He did not preach withdrawal from the world, but active participation in it. They preached a similar message, only Yeshua did it better, using evocative language, striking examples and impactful stories. And while John spoke of hellfire and repentance, Yeshua emphasised forgiveness, humility and love.

---

[111] Matt 21:31-32

THE KINGDOM OF G __ D

83. Yeshua's mission was to proclaim the coming of the Kingdom

When you read carefully, one fact jumps out at you from almost every chapter of the Synoptic Gospels. It's often overlooked and sometimes downplayed, but once spotted and its significance is understood, it casts a long shadow over the whole of the New Testament. It was the subject of most of his parables and sayings and is acknowledged by most Bible scholars.

It is this: Yeshua's chief message, the one he had taken from John the Baptist, was that the Kingdom of G_d[112] was on its way. *Soon.* The world *in its present form* was about to be transformed. G_d would take direct charge and establish the Kingdom, not in some afterlife but in this one. The Son of Man would then be at G_d's right hand. People must ground themselves in G_d and learn to live right because judgement would immediately follow. Only those who had changed their ways (repented) and met the required standards would be allowed to enter.

This was not some far-distant event; it would happen within a generation. Yeshua was unequivocal about this. 'Truly I tell you,' he says in the First Gospel, 'there are some standing here who will not taste death until they see that the Kingdom of G_d has come with power.'[113] 'The time is fulfilled, and the Kingdom of

---

112 The First Gospel calls it the 'Kingdom of God', so, on the whole, do Paul and 'Luke'. The Fourth Gospel barely mentions the term at all. Matthew's Gospel calls it the 'Kingdom of Heaven' since Jews avoided speaking the name of G_d.

113 Mark 9:1

G_d has come near; repent, and believe in the good news.'[114] He reaffirmed it in his Last Supper speech, telling his disciples, 'I will never again drink of this fruit of the vine until that day when I drink it with you in my Father's kingdom.'[115] He didn't mean a kingdom somewhere else, but right here on Earth.

84. His followers took him literally

The Kingdom was not a strange idea for the Jews; the Hebrew Scriptures made it quite clear that G_d would intervene whenever necessary to get the chosen people back on-track, and the day was coming soon. Paul of Tarsus echoed these teachings and the early Christians took them literally.

Now, nearly two thousand years later, it is clear that Yeshua, Paul, John the Baptist, the Synoptic Gospel writers and the rest were mistaken, or to put it bluntly, wrong. Indeed it was clear that by the end of the 1ˢᵗ Century that the Kingdom was not coming, which is why it is almost entirely missing from the Fourth Gospel.

85. Yeshua was an eschatologist

For more than a century, biblical scholars have believed that Yeshua was primarily an apocalyptic prophet who was put to death by the Romans for sedition when he claimed he would be king of the Jews in a future kingdom. In other words, he was an eschatologist - one who believes the world is about to end or be radically transformed. But unfortunately the scholarly view has not reached the people in the pews and this has led to some serious misunderstandings about the gospels' messages. Whether Yeshua

---

[114]   Mark 1:15

[115]   Matthew 26:29

looked much beyond the arrival of the Kingdom is questionable since all the errors and inequities would disappear.

The implications of the eschatological view are profound. It's reasonable to turn your attention away from worldly concerns such as family, money and where your next meal is coming from if the world is about to end because they would no longer have any value in the new order. But if life is to continue as it is, then these things are important for survival.

Nor was there any point in campaigning for political change or fighting the Romans since all injustice would disappear when the world was transformed. It was far more important to get own your house in order so you would not be refused entry to the Kingdom.

86. The gospels don't define the 'Kingdom of G_d'

The gospels don't define the Kingdom of G_d. Perhaps the authors felt that their readership already understood the term and there was no need for detailed explanation. Instead, Yeshua explains it in parables, short sayings and analogies.

- The Kingdom of G_d would be a new world order – not an afterlife, but a transformation on Earth. Poverty, sickness and injustice would be swept away, and there would be no temptation or wickedness.
- It was close at hand and within everyone's reach.[116] G_d wanted everyone to enter. Every 'lost sheep' would be found and carried 'home'[117]. And, according to Paul of Tarsus, even the dead would rise and take their place[118].

---

[116] Luke 17: 20-21
[117] Luke 15:3-7
[118] 1 Thessalonians 4:15-17

- People would be selected for the Kingdom according to their attitude and conduct – the humble and meek before the pompous and self-righteous. Only the highest moral standards would be acceptable. They must love G-d and each other, and show forgiveness, compassion, initiative, generosity and humility to their fellow humans – and that was just for starters! They must use their G_d-given talents to the full, and take as much pleasure from another being chosen for the Kingdom as themselves.
- The Kingdom would bring an inner transformation, like yeast which causes one's spiritual faculties to 'rise'.
- It was like a great pearl or treasure buried in a field, so valuable that is worth selling all one has and buying the whole field.[119]
- Humans couldn't make it happen. All they could do was prepare themselves so they would be ready when the time came.[120] Then, in Paul of Tarsus's words, 'We shall not all sleep, but we shall all be changed. In a moment, in the twinkling of an eye.'[121]

86. Yeshua never claimed that he would establish the Kingdom himself

Yeshua was initially reluctant to make any claims about himself in the Synoptic Gospels. He never claimed that he would establish the Kingdom but prepare the people for its coming. He was simply the facilitator.

But then his teachings about the Kingdom changed during his year-long ministry. Early on he spoke of the Kingdom in the

---

[119]   Matthew 13:31-48
[120]   Mark 13:4-37
[121]   1 Corinthians 15:51

future; later he said that the change was already happening. There would be a period of turmoil then Jerusalem would be destroyed by the gentiles as predicted in the Hebrew Scriptures. The disciples must proclaim the good news but would face hardship. After the torment, the Son of Man would come in glory. Once the kingdom was established, he, Yeshua, would be at G_d's right hand[122] and the disciples would each rule over (or judge) one of the restored twelve tribes of Israel.

87. The world was supposed to end at midnight on 31st December 1999

Imagine if someone appeared today claiming that the world was about to end, and he would lead his followers into a new era? Well, actually there are such people, and apart from their closest followers, most of us consider them mad. I met one such person just before the turn of the millennium. She believed that the world would end at midnight on 31st December 1999. A spaceship would swoop down from behind Uranus, collect the faithful from the top of a mountain in the Rockies and carry them off to a new life on a distant planet. I have no idea what happened to her, but I wonder how she felt when she woke up on January 1st 2000.

If Yeshua were alive today, would we think of him as a lunatic like her?

88. As the 1st Century progressed, Yeshua's prediction began to look mistaken

The fact that the world was not transformed in his lifetime, nor his disciples', nor Paul's, nor the gospel writers', in fact, not

---

[122]   Mark 13:24-7

ever – is one of the contradictions that has beset Christianity for nearly two thousand years. This was not just disappointing, but the breaking of a solemn promise Yeshua had made to his people. How could the Son of G_d break his promise?

As the 1st Century progressed, Yeshua's prediction of the imminent arrival of the Kingdom began to look more and more mistaken. Indeed, the Third Gospel, written in the 9th or 10th decade, played it down and the Fourth Gospel barely mentions it at all. It had unquestionably been superseded by events. Christians realised that this made them look ridiculous and made excuses. The author of the Second Letter attributed to Peter (but not written by him) felt the need to smooth over the kingdom's non-appearance. 'Do not ignore this one fact, beloved,' he wrote, 'that with the Lord one day is like a thousand years, and a thousand years like one day.'[123]

August Friedrich Gfrörer (1803-1861)[124] described Christianity as a system which only maintained itself by force, after having commended itself to antiquity 'by the hope of the mystic kingdom of the future world and having ruled the Middle Ages by the fear of the same future.'

Why doesn't the church have more to say about Yeshua's eschatological leanings? Is it because they worry that bringing it to people's attention would make Yeshua's core teachings seem irrelevant in our time? After all, he was wrong. The world was not transformed within the lifetime of his disciples. G_d did not appear, and neither did he.

---

[123]   2 Cephas 3:8
[124]   Quoted in Albert Schweitzer, *The Quest of the Historical Jesus,* pg 163.

89. It's not unusual for religious people to believe that their prophet came into the world in a miraculous way

It's not unusual for religious people to believe that their prophet or guru came into the world in a miraculous way. Christians are no exception. The stories of Yeshua's birth are integral to their religion. Christmas is celebrated annually around the world and is second only to Easter in importance, although the Easter festival has less appeal.

The gospels are far from congruent, though. For a start, two of the gospels don't mention Yeshua's birth at all; the Nativity stories re-enacted every December are based on just the Second and Third Gospels, and their accounts are so different it's hard to believe they're referring to the same events. The only thing they have in common is the supposed location, Bethlehem, and their wish to portray Yeshua's birth as a profoundly important event with supernatural overtones. 'Matthew' was also concerned to link it to Yeshua's Jewish heritage and the Hebrew prophecies.

90. There were many myths concerning a virgin-born, resurrected god-man

There were many myths concerning a virgin-born, resurrected god-man across the Middle East at that time.[125] In Egypt the god-man was Osiris. His mother was a mortal virgin. He was born in a cowshed before three shepherds, turned water into wine at a

---

[125] Source: Timothy Freke and Cephas Gandy, *The Jesus Mysteries*'

marriage ceremony, rode triumphantly on a donkey while people waved palm leaves to honour him, died, and on the third day rose from the dead and ascended to heaven in glory. Remember – this was not Yeshua but Osiris, nearly six centuries before the gospels were written!

A virgin birth would have appeared even more amazing in the 1st Century since they didn't know that women produce eggs which are fertilised by the father. They thought that the woman merely nurtured the man's seed until the baby was born. That's why women didn't count when determining descent.

91. The early Christians had no knowledge of Yeshua's 'miraculous' conception and birth

The early Christian community seems to have had no knowledge of the Christmas stories. Even the two gospel authors who mention them make no reference to them after the first two chapters. Yeshua's birth is not referred to in either 'Matthew' or 'Luke's' accounts of his adult ministry, trial, crucifixion or resurrection, making some scholars think that these chapters were added later. Besides, there is no mention of the miraculous nativity anywhere else in the New Testament: not in the earliest gospel, 'Mark', nor in Paul's letters which pre-date 'Mark'; not in the Fourth Gospel, Acts of the Apostles or the later letters. Don't you think that these other authors would have mentioned these events? Did they not know of them, or did they not consider them important? This seems unlikely. The New Testament tells us that Paul spent a couple of weeks with Yeshua's disciple Cephas[126] and brother Tiago in Jerusalem – are we to believe that the subject was never raised, *if they happened*?

---

[126] The Aramaic name of Simon Peter.

Nowhere in the gospels does Yeshua make any reference to his birth, not even in the Fourth which devotes verse after verse to him talking about himself. Nor is there anything in the New Testament to suggest that his mother Maryām acknowledged the miraculous conception when her son was grown up and active in the world. Curious indeed! Needless to say these inconsistencies are never pointed out from pulpits, raised in discussion or mentioned in church literature. Why not?

92. The Hebrew prophecy of a virgin birth is based on a mistranslation

The Second and Third Gospels tell us that Yeshua's mother was a virgin at the time of his conception and that this had been prophesied in the Hebrew Scriptures. But this particular prophecy was a mistranslation of a passage from Isaiah written in Hebrew in the 8th Century BCE[127]. Modern translations[128] read as follows: 'Look, the *young woman* is with child and shall bear a son.....' Older, less accurate translations (including the King James Bible) say, 'Behold a *virgin* shall conceive...' Moreover, when you read the passage in Isaiah it is clear that the author was predicting something that would happen to a King Ahaz in his own time, not 800 years later! Regrettably, the incorrect version continues to be widely used, compounding the error.

93. The cult of the Virgin Mary originated in the 3rd and 4th Centuries

The belief that Yeshua's mother was a virgin was not enshrined into church thinking until at least a century after his death and

---

[127]   Isaiah 7:14

[128]   E.g. New Revised Standard Version, 1989, Oxford University Press

was later popularised in the 4th Century by the towering figure of Bishop Augustine of Hippo (354-430 CE). The cult of the Virgin Mary was cemented in church dogma at the Council of Nicaea in 325CE. It played no part in the religion at the time of the early apostles simply because they knew nothing of it.

The idea of a virgin birth appealed strongly to Bishop Augustine. Since Yeshua was divine, he argued, he could not have come into the world through sinful means. Sex was sinful, therefore his mother must have been a virgin when he was conceived.

Some Christians believe that Maryām remained a lifelong virgin, but this is directly contradicted in the Second Gospel: 'Joseph... took her (Mary) as his wife but had no marital relations with her until she had borne a son.'[129] In other words, she did have normal marital relations with her husband after Yeshua was born. Moreover, there is no indication in the gospels that Maryām was revered in Biblical times.

As time went by, some theologians started to believe that she too was immaculately conceived and was eventually taken into heaven in bodily form since there's no mention of her death and burial in the Bible. Nevertheless, despite its questionable foundations, Maryām is seen by many as the perfect embodiment of womanhood and her veneration is a major plank of the Catholic faith. So strong is this notion that there have many been reported sightings of her ever since, at Lourdes for example.

---

[129]   Matthew 1:24-25

94. There was no reason for Yeshua's parents to be in Bethlehem for his birth

The Second and Third Gospels say that Yeshua was born in Bethlehem, a small town close to Jerusalem. It was especially important for 'Matthew' that Yeshua was seen to come from Bethlehem, the birthplace of the great King David, since he was keen to portray Yeshua as the fulfilment of the ancient scriptures and the prophet Micah had foreseen the Messiah being born there.[130] 'Matthew' says that Yehosef and Maryām were already in Bethlehem when the birth took place, presumably living there.[131] The author therefore had no need to explain why this young couple from Nazareth decided to journey eighty miles through hostile territory, Samaria, to give birth; that trumped-up story came from 'Luke'.

The vehicle chosen by 'Luke' was a Roman Census which required every citizen to return to their ancestral home. Because Yehosef was said to be a descendent of King David, this meant Bethlehem. It's a good story, but it simply isn't true. The author gets his facts in a complete muddle. He states that Quirinius was Governor of Syria at the time of the census, but Quirinius did not take power in Syria until 6 CE, ten years after the death of King Herod. Moreover historians have been unable to find any records of a census in that region at the time of Yeshua's birth, despite the Romans being assiduous record keepers. Indeed, no census took place there between the years 10 BCE and 6 CE.

There was a census in 6 CE, but it did not include Galilee since Quirinius had no jurisdiction there. Moreover, it did not require people to travel. It would have made no sense for all Jews, scattered around the Roman Empire and beyond, to return to their place

---

[130] Micah 5:2
[131] Matthew 2:1

of their family origins. And not even the Romans would have insisted that a heavily pregnant woman travel from Nazareth to Bethlehem on a donkey.

Incidentally, the First Gospel makes no reference to Bethlehem, while the Fourth reports an incident in which a crowd doubted that he was the Messiah *precisely because he did not come from Bethlehem*, but from Galilee[132]. Galilee was simply not the sort of place where the Jews expected to find their Messiah. Even so, the historical evidence along with two of the gospels strongly suggests that Yeshua was born in the town where he grew up, Nazareth.

95. If Yehosef was not Yeshua's father, then Yeshua was not a descendent of King David

If Yeshua was to be the fulfilment of the ancient Hebrew prophecies it was important that he be seen as a descendant of the great King David. David lived around 1000 BCE – at least forty generations earlier. In the normal course of events, if every descendent reached adulthood and bore two children, David would have had more descendants after forty generations than the entire population of the world!

To prove his point, the Second Gospel compiled a lineage that traced Yeshua back to the great king through his mother's husband, Yehosef[133]. Yehosef was not, of course, his biological father according to the same author! Moreover, the Third Gospel also has a genealogy[134] and it's quite different. Compare them for yourself!

---

[132] John 7:40–42
[133] Matthew 1:1–17
[134] Luke 3:23–38

Paul of Tarsus, who made no claims for a miraculous birth in any of his letters, also stated without proof that Yeshua was 'descended from David, according to the flesh'.[135] Yeshua is referred to as Son of David throughout the Synoptic Gospels, though he never made this claim for himself, and there is no reference at all to the term in 'John'.

96. Nativity scenes should not show cows, donkeys or angels because they aren't mentioned in the Bible!

Most people are familiar with the nativity scene set in a stable. The 'holy family' are surrounded by farm animals, shepherds, angels and the three wise men bearing gifts of gold, frankincense and myrrh, all paying tribute to the new 'king'. But even the Catholic Church doesn't accept this version of events – interestingly, in November 2012 Pope Benedict remarked that nativity scenes should not show cows, donkeys or a choir of angels because they aren't mentioned in the Bible!

Moreover, 'Luke's' shepherds could not possibly have attended the birth at the same time as the wise men. According to the author the shepherd left their sheep immediately at the behest of an angel and went straight to the new-born Messiah lying in a manger, a trough or an open box in which feed for livestock is placed. Fair enough, but it would have taken weeks for 'Matthew's' wise men to arrive from a foreign country. They are said to have followed a star which led them to Bethlehem and somehow hovered low enough over the place where the infant was for it to be identified. And what happened to the gold, frankincense and myrrh they brought as gifts?[136] They were extremely valuable. If Maryām and

---

[135] Romans 1:3

[136] In Matthew's account, the wise men bear the same gifts as are stated in a Zoroastrian myth. This is likely to have been added centuries later.

Yehosef had actually had these things they could have sold them and lived the rest of their lives in comfort.

97. 'Matthew' and 'Luke's' birth stories can't both be right

According to the Third Gospel[137], Yeshua was circumcised on the eighth day according to the custom. Two elderly people, Simeon and Anna, came to worship him and the family then returned to Nazareth. But the Second Gospel says that they fled to Egypt to avoid an order from King Herod that all new born Jewish boys in Bethlehem be killed[138]. There's no historical record of any such decree, and no evidence of any slaughter of Jewish babies at that time. More likely it was the author's imaginative way of linking Yeshua's birth to a passage in the Hebrew Scriptures in which G_d says, 'Out of Egypt I called my son.'[139]

So did they flee to Egypt or return directly to Nazareth? They can't both be right.

Were 'Matthew' and 'Luke' barefaced liars? No more than many novelists, filmmakers, public relations experts and journalists who embellish a little to make a point. They wanted others to share their beliefs about Yeshua, and saw no harm in using a little artistic licence. In the longer term they helped to bring Yeshua's life and teachings to a wider audience, but, along with the Apostle Paul's teachings, turned people's attention away from *what he taught* to *who he was*. And this is perhaps their greatest legacy.

---

[137]   Luke 2:39

[138]   Matthew 2:13-15

[139]   Hosea 11:1

98. The December Christmas celebrations date from 354 CE

No-one knows the exact date of Yeshua's birth, but we can be certain it wasn't the 25th December. Traditionally Western Christians celebrate on this day each year; in the Orthodox Churches Christmas Day is 7th January.

In 137 CE, the Bishop of Rome ordered the birth to be celebrated annually, but there was no consensus over the precise date. The December nativity celebrations date from 354 CE, to coincide with the Pagan midwinter festival held throughout the Roman Empire. So paradoxically Christians commemorate the birth of their saviour on the date of ancient Pagan festival!

In the 6th Century, the Catholic Church introduced Advent, with rituals and sacraments on the four Sundays leading up to Christmas and the Midnight Mass on Christmas Eve. The Christmas Tree probably has its origins in 8th Century Scandinavia. The use of mistletoe came from the Druids, and holly and ivy from the Saxons.

Nowadays the Christmas holiday is an opportunity to take a much needed break, cheering people up in the depths of the Northern Hemisphere winter. It's also a selling opportunity for commercial interests at a time of year when consumer resistance is low. In 2010, despite the worst world recession in living memory, rampant displays of gluttony and greed were as much in evidence as ever. That year the average adult in the UK spent over £412 on gifts and the UK population as a whole spent a staggering £1.2 billion on *unwanted* Christmas presents – enough to fund the nation's charities for 10 years!

99. It is unnecessary to believe in the virgin birth to be a good Christian

When the newly appointed Anglican Bishop of Durham, Dr David Jenkins, said he did not believe the gospel birth stories in the early 1980s and that such belief was not necessary to be a good Christian, he attracted huge publicity and was widely chastised in Christian circles. But there was nothing new in what he said – he was merely expressing a view that had long existed among scholars. For example, Dr Albert Schweitzer wrote in his studious text *The Quest of the Historical Jesus* (published in 1906): 'The histories of Yeshua's birth are not literary versions of a tradition, but literary inventions.'

HIS STORY

100. A dependable account of Yeshua's adult life is not possible because the only sources we have are unreliable

As we've observed, it's hard to piece together a completely dependable account of Yeshua's adult life because the only detailed sources we have – the gospels – are contradictory, confused and unreliable for all the reasons given (and there's more to come). But they're the best we have, because they're *all* we have.

The following sections draw heavily on the gospels and gospel scholarship, commenting on Yeshua's story and pointing out some of the most important contradictions and historical inaccuracies.

MISSION IMPOSSIBLE

101. Forty days in the wilderness

The Synoptics say that Yeshua spent forty days and nights in the wilderness after his baptism and was tempted by Satan, the devil. 'Mark's' account is, typically, short and to the point – just two verses saying he was with wild beasts and attended by angels.[140] 'Matthew's' is embellished by quotations from the Hebrew Scriptures and so is 'Luke's'. The Fourth Gospel says nothing about it.

It would be impossible for a human being to survive forty days in intense heat without food or water[141] while fighting off 'wild beasts'. Equally implausible are the accounts in the Second Gospel of Satan trying to tempt Yeshua into turning stones into bread, throwing himself off the temple pinnacle and worshipping Satan in exchange for all the kingdoms in the world[142]. These stories bear all the hallmarks of allegory - unless Yeshua was hallucinating!

On emerging from the wilderness, the gospels say Yeshua's year-long mission began. Or was it three years? Or four? The gospels don't agree – the Synoptics imply only one, the Fourth at least three.

---

[140] Mark 1:12-13
[141] See Luke 4:2
[142] Matthew 4:1-11. Luke's account is similar.

102. Satan was invented in the 5th Century BCE

Most Christians believe there are two powers ruling us, G_d and a potent adversary, Satan. Satan's task is to tempt us to turn away from obeying G_d's will. He[143] is pure evil personified. He puts ideas into people's heads which they can accept and act upon or reject.

There is no mention of Satan or the devil in the Pentateuch. Satan first appeared in the Hebrew Scriptures in the 5th Century BCE to explain how a loving G_d could have broken a solemn promise and allowed the destruction of the Jerusalem Temple in 586 BCE. Hassatan, 'the Adversary', grew in importance down the centuries. By the time Revelation was written, he had become a significant figure for Jews and Christians and remains so to this day.

The church teaches that we are cut off from G_d and refused salvation[144] if we succumb to Satan's influence, but believing that Yeshua's death and resurrection atones for our sins, prevents Satan from having his way so we are saved from eternal damnation. This is, of course, Paul of Tarsus's teaching, not Yeshua's.

According to many Christians, Satan's greatest trick is persuading us he doesn't exist.

---

[143] Satan like G_d, is usually portrayed as male.

[144] According to Prof Marcus Borg, the original meaning of 'salvation' had nothing to do with going to heaven in a future life, but meant 'rescue from harm' or 'personal transformation' in this.

103. In Hebrew culture, twelve was an important number

On emerging from the wilderness, Yeshua attracted disciples, or, if you take the gospels literally, *appointed* them. The gospels say there were twelve in his inner circle, but historians give this little credence; there were probably never exactly twelve. In Hebrew culture, twelve was an important number. It represented the twelve tribes that formed the original nation of Israel, eleven of which had long since disappeared. Yeshua promised, like John the Baptist before him, that they would be restored in the coming Kingdom of G_d. Each disciple would be placed at the head of one of these tribes and would be its judge when the Kingdom arrived.

Yeshua intended to instruct his inner circle so they would train others, but they were slow learners; he had to repeat his message to them over and over again in private, using different stories and examples. He wanted followers who could spread the message. He urged them to go out into the people and 'as you go, proclaim the good news: the Kingdom of Heaven has come near.'[145] Within a few months, the gospels say there were disciples in every town and village in Galilee.[146]

Yeshua's close followers unquestionably included women, but none of them are listed as disciples in the gospels. Some of his female followers were sufficiently wealthy to provide for the group from their own resources.[147] That was unusual, since Jewish women had no legal status at that time. They could not officially earn or inherit property, only accept gifts from their men folk.

---

[145]   Matthew 10:8

[146]   'Luke' says 70 more disciples were later appointed. (Symbolically – and coincidentally - there were 70 nations in the known world at that time).

[147]   Luke 8:3

104. The gospels disagree over how the disciples were recruited

Each gospel attempts to explain how the disciples were recruited. There is little congruence between them.

- 'Luke' would have us believe that Yeshua arranged a massive catch of fish to impress a group of fishermen who had had a barren day. They dropped everything, abandoned their families and immediately followed him, just like that![148]
- 'Mark' and 'Matthew' also say he recruited fishermen but make no mention of a massive catch.
- 'John' makes no mention of fishing and hints that Yeshua recruited from John the Baptist's disciples[149]. He doesn't even agree with the others on the names!

105. Yeshua expected the highest standards of his followers

Yeshua was uncompromising in the standards expected of his followers. They must treat others right, feed the hungry, comfort the sick and visit the imprisoned; be compassionate, humble, honest, respectful, gentle and loving towards others. Of his closest disciples he expected even more. They must demonstrate their willingness to:

- Put Yeshua first, even above their families.
- Trust G_d completely.
- Be hated and never retaliate.
- Be happy when rejected.
- Postpone gratification, trusting that their rewards would come later.
- Love and pray for those who ill-treat them.

---

[148] Luke 5:1-11
[149] John 1:35-45

- Sell everything they have and give the money to the poor.
- Be defenceless as sheep among wolves.
- Be as wise as serpents and innocent as doves.
- Be joyful, even when persecuted.

In exchange they would get to judge the re-formed twelve tribes of Israel in the coming Kingdom of G_d, enjoy the mutual love and respect of other disciples, recognition as one of G_d's representatives, the support of the Holy Spirit, and eternal life.

106. Scholars regard Yeshua's teachings in the Synoptic Gospels as the most accurate material

The teachings of Yeshua in the Synoptic Gospels are probably the most accurately recorded and reliable material in the New Testament from a historical point of view. They are so original, so impactful and in places so memorable that anyone less than a great spiritual teacher could not have made them up, but we can't be sure Yeshua delivered them in the given format.

The Fourth Gospel discourses are quite different. They are long and wordy, and best regarded as literary creations in which the author expressed his theology using the long-dead Yeshua as his mouthpiece.

To get his message across to the poor and underprivileged of Galilee and the Jerusalem elites alike he used six main methods:

I.   Discourses and sayings
II. Confrontation
III. Questions and answers
IV. Parables
V.   Miracles
VI. Actions

YESHUA'S TEACHING ACTIVITIES

107. The best-known discourse is the 'Sermon on the Mount'

The gospels are rich in lengthy speeches, short, pithy sayings and memorable stories with powerful messages. The gospel discourses were constructed to educate and inspire the early Christians. The best-known is the Sermon on the Mount. There are two versions, one in the Second Gospel, another in the Third, but there's no reference to it in the First or Fourth.

However, the two versions are quite different: 'Matthew's' version extends to over a hundred verses, 'Luke's' just thirty two. 'Matthew's' Sermon is delivered from 'up a mountain'[150] although strictly speaking there are no mountains in Galilee, 'Luke's' 'from a level place'[151]. Perhaps the author of 'Matthew' intended the mountain to represent a high place of spiritual consciousness rather than a geographical place, or it was 'Matthew's' attempt to link Yeshua with the legend of Moses delivering the Ten Commandments on Mount Sinai[152].

Many scholars believe 'Luke's' version more authentic. 'Matthew's' is very likely to be a composite of teachings arranged by the author from material delivered many times to different audiences in different places, then passed down by word of mouth (and perhaps in the Book of Q). Similar passages also occur throughout the First Gospel and the Gnostic Gospel of Thomas.

---

[150] Matthew 5:1
[151] Luke 6:17-49
[152] Exodus Ch 20

The full text of 'Matthew's' Sermon on the Mount appears in Chapters Five, Six and Seven of the Second Gospel. The teachings are divided into five sections, all intended to show the way to the Kingdom of G_d (or Kingdom of Heaven, as 'Matthew' generally prefers to call it):

I.   The Beatitudes[153] – nine sayings that begin with 'Blessed are....' intended to comfort the poor and suffering. The Beatitudes turned the world on its head since people considered impure under Jewish Law would be blessed in the coming Kingdom.

II. Guidelines for living. Yeshua told his audiences that thoughts and words have the same effect as physical actions, and that observing religious practices is of little use if you are in dispute with another person. He warned against judging others, adultery, divorce, swearing oaths and seeking revenge. He urged them to put aside anything that would prevent them entering the Kingdom and love their neighbours and enemies equally. He said that all who seek spiritual wisdom will receive it and restated the Golden Rule from the Hebrew Scriptures: 'In everything, do to others as you would have them do to you.' Finally, he urged that it is not enough to know the truth, you must live it.

III. Instructions on prayer, fasting and giving alms. 'Go into your room alone and shut the door,' he said, 'and pray to your Father who is in secret; and your Father who sees in secret will reward you.' Then he recommended a form of words now known as the Lord's Prayer. A modern translation is:

Our Father in heaven, hallowed by your name.

Your kingdom come.

---

[153]   Derived from the Latin 'beatus,' which means blessed or happy.

Your will be done, on earth as it is in heaven.

Give us this day our daily bread.

And forgive us our debts, as we also have forgiven our debtors.

And do not bring us to the time of trial, but rescue us from the evil one.[154]

IV. Teachings on money and material prosperity. Yeshua warned against becoming obsessed with 'treasures on earth' and assured his audience that G_d would provide everything they needed if they lived correctly. 'Strive first for the kingdom and its righteousness[155] and all these things will be given to you as well.'[156]

V. Warnings about hypocrisy and false prophets, reiterating some of the instructions in the Torah.

'Matthew's' Sermon on the Mount is one of the most important passages in the New Testament, if not the entire Bible. It is instructive, thought-provoking, challenging and inspiring, especially when we reflect on the meaning behind the words rather than taking every phrase literally. For an enlightened summary I highly recommend Dr Eric Butterworth's book, 'Discover the Power Within You,'[157] a modern classic.

---

[154] Luke's version of the Lord's Prayer is different and does not appear in his Sermon from a Level Place.

[155] According to Prof Borg, 'righteousness' may be better translated as 'justice'.

[156] Matthew 6:33

[157] Dr Eric Butterworth, 'Discover the Power Within You,' HarperSanFrancisco, 1992, ISBN 0-06-250115-1.

108. We don't know if all of Yeshua's sayings were meant to be taken literally

We don't know which of Yeshua's gospel sayings were meant to be taken literally. 'It is easier for a camel to go through the eye of a needle than for someone who is rich to enter the Kingdom of God,' is a case in point.[158] On the face of it, Yeshua is simply saying that it is impossible for a rich man to enter the Kingdom of G_d. But was he smiling when he said it or was his expression serious? Was he angry? And did he really mean a camel? The Aramaic words for 'camel' and 'rope' sounded alike, so he may have meant passing a *rope* through the eye of a needle. This sounds much more likely, but we'll never know for sure.

Another example – and this has cost lives – was attributed to the resurrected Yeshua in the addendum to the First Gospel: those who believe 'will pick up snakes in their hands, and if they drink any deadly thing, it will not hurt them.[159] If Yeshua actually said this, was he really suggesting that people should drink poison and pick up snakes to prove their faith? We'll never know, but some evangelical Christians in the USA today act on these words. They handle poisonous snakes, and if they are bitten take it as a sign that their faith is lacking. Many have died.

109. Yeshua made enemies among his own people

Yeshua made enemies, but if we believe the gospels they were not primarily the Romans; his most bitter enemies were the movers and shakers among his own people, the Jewish religious leaders. Although the Romans ruled with a rod of iron, the Jews were granted a large degree of autonomy in social and religious

---

[158]   Mark 10:25
[159]   Mark 16:18. Luke 10:19 has Yeshua making a similar statement.)

matters. This put a great deal of influence in the hands of the hereditary elite who ran the Jerusalem Temple, the Sadducees. Yeshua was appalled that this self-seeking aristocratic class were more concerned with protecting their own privileges than helping the common people.

Built into the temple system was the requirement for every Jew to pay taxes to the priests if they wished to enjoy temple privileges. These payments were even more unpopular than the extortionate taxes paid to the Romans, and since most of the Jewish population couldn't afford them, they were effectively excluded from their own religion.

Did Yeshua also make enemies among the Romans? We can't be sure, but it seems likely. We know the gospels were sanitised after the Romans adopted Christianity as their official religion. Obviously they didn't want their saviour portrayed as being in conflict with the Romans of his day.

110. The gospels describe repeated clashes between Yeshua and the Pharisees

The Pharisees were a hated sect who saw themselves as protectors of Jewish Law and believed that all 613 precepts of the Torah should be observed to the letter. They seemed to follow him around, frequently popping up and challenging Yeshua's teachings and behaviour. In return, Yeshua seemed to delight in confronting them and putting them down, giving him an opportunity to expand on his teachings.

Yeshua also clashed with the scribes, whose role was to record and interpret the legal material laid down in the Torah. He thought they missed the point of the Law and lacked compassion. For example, they were quick to condemn anyone who broke the food laws, but had nothing to say about the plight of the starving.

Among the behaviours to which the Pharisees objected were:

- Teaching that all were equal before G_d, whether or not they observed the Law.
- Mixing with people they considered unclean – the poor, women (including prostitutes), tax collectors, outcasts, lepers, beggars and so on.
- Disregarding the rules forbidding working and healing on the Sabbath day.
- Toning down the food laws. He said that it is not what goes into a person that defiles them, but what comes out.[160]
- Telling people that their sins were forgiven. Pharisees believed only priests could ask G_d to forgive sins.
- Beginning his teaching with, 'I say unto you...'. The prophets of old always began, 'Thus says the Lord G_d...'[161] but Yeshua claimed this authority for himself.

Yeshua only confronted the Temple rulers, the Sadducees, towards the end of his life, but had frequent contact with the Pharisees and scribes. Wherever he went, they harangued him, and in return he directed his most stunning ripostes at them. For instance, they asked why he mixed with the unclean, and he explained that these were the very people who needed the most help.[162]

---

[160] Mark 7:15
[161] E.g. Isaiah 7:7
[162] Mark 2:16-17

111. Yeshua was a master of questions and answers

Yeshua was a master at the question and answer method used by teachers everywhere. Sometimes, the gospels say, people would ask a question to try and trick him but he always had a clever answer for them. For example, towards the end of his life some Sadducees challenged him with a question about the afterlife (Sadducees did not believe in life after death). They asked if a woman had had seven husbands in this life, whose wife would she be in the afterlife? Yeshua told them they didn't know the scriptures. He said. 'When they rise from the dead, they are like angels in heaven, and angels don't marry.' He added pointedly, 'G_d is not the god of the dead, but of the living'[163].

112. All Yeshua's parables were original

Parables are short simple stories with a moral. Unlike many of Yeshua's sayings which were 'borrowed' from the Hebrew Scriptures, all his parables were original although some were enhanced by the gospel writers and/or subsequent editors to clarify their meaning. There is nothing like Yeshua's parables elsewhere in the Hebrew, Greek or Latin traditions.

The Synoptics record over thirty parables but the Fourth Gospel doesn't mention any of them. Not one! Perhaps the best-known are the Good Samaritan[164] and the Prodigal Son[165], although the Sower,[166] the Lost Sheep[167] and the Talents[168] are also

---

[163] Mark 12:18-27

[164] Luke 10:29-37

[165] Luke 15:11-32

[166] Matthew 13:3-8

[167] Matthew 18:12-14

[168] Matthew 25:14-30

well-known. Where the parables are duplicated there are usually slight variations, with 'Mark's' versions the most concise. Some are crystal clear in meaning, some are obscure. But their main message is invariably the imminent coming of the Kingdom, what it would be like and who would be allowed to enter.

113. The gospels report more than thirty miracles, mainly healings and exorcisms

The gospels tell us that Yeshua was known in Galilee as a worker of miracles. This is verified to some extent by the historian, Josephus, who commented on his reputation as a healer; indeed, his fame at the time may have come primarily from these activities. He was not unique in this respect, though; there were many supposed miracle workers in 1st Century Palestine and Yeshua's miracles were not so different from those attributed to certain others at that time, such as Honi, Hanina and Eleazar.

More than thirty miracles are featured in the gospels, mainly healings and exorcisms but also miracles which seemed to transcend the natural order of things, like turning water into wine, walking on water, calming a storm and raising the dead. The Synoptics are brimming with miracles, but they are barely mentioned by Paul of Tarsus, and the Fourth Gospel lists only four: turning water into wine, curing a blind man with his saliva, the raising of Lazarus from the dead and healing a nobleman's son.

114. Yeshua used a combination of healing methods

The twenty miraculous healings described in the gospels include a variety of diseases and congenital defects, demonic possessions, a severed ear and three accounts of people being raised from the dead. The authors say that Yeshua used five main healing methods and sometimes a combination of these. In every case, the effect was instantaneous:

1. Healing by command: Many of the healings involved a direct command spoken with authority. For example, he told a man with a withered hand to 'Stretch out your hand'.[169] The hand was immediately restored.

2. Healing by touch. On one occasion, Yeshua was not even aware that the touch had taken place.[170] One of the most dramatic is reported in the Third Gospel. Someone cut off the ear of the High Priest's slave with a sword as they were arresting Yeshua in the Garden of Gethsemane. Yeshua touched the ear and healed it. [171] (There is no mention of this incident in the other gospels.)

3. There are three reported instances in which Yeshua used his own saliva to bring about healing.[172]

4. Distance healing: the gospels say that Yeshua did not need to be with the recipient to bring about a cure. 'John' says he healed a royal official's dying son,[173] 'Matthew' a Roman centurion's paralysed servant[174] and 'Mark' a young girl possessed by demons – all without seeing them in person.

5. The raising of Lazarus is the most dramatic miracle of all. It appears only in the Fourth Gospel[175]. The writer claims that Lazarus had been dead in his tomb for four days and was beginning to stink when Yeshua ordered him to

---

[169] Mark 3: 1-12
[170] Luke 8:43-48
[171] Luke 22:50-51
[172] Mark 7:32-36, Mark 8:22-26, John 9:6-7
[173] John 4:46-54
[174] Matthew 8:5-13 Mark 7:24
[175] John 11:1-44

come out. Lazarus emerged, his hands, feet and face still bound with the burial cloth. Yeshua then delivered one of those lengthy monologues for which 'John's' Gospel is noted. If this were true (and barely any bible experts believe that it is), wouldn't you expect the other gospel writers to devote a paragraph or two to it? And why did Paul not think it worth mentioning in his letters?

The story of Lazarus is constructed around one of the New Testament's most famous sayings which is widely quoted by proselyting Christians everywhere: 'I am the resurrection and the life. Those who believe in me, even though they die, will live, and everyone who lives and believes in me will never die.' [176] One suspects that this – not providing a factual account - was its real purpose.

115. Yeshua did not regard his healing abilities as exclusive to him

The Fourth Gospel made it clear that Yeshua regarded healing as something that anyone with faith could do. He said, 'The one who believes in me will also do the works that I do and, in fact, will do greater works than these, because I am going to the Father.'[177] He urged his disciples to go forth and heal and gave them instructions.

Many Christians do not appear to understand this; they believe that only Yeshua, saints and perhaps the official representatives of the Church can access G_d's power to heal. But we should not be so sceptical. There have been countless healers down the ages,

---

[176] John 11:25-26
[177] John 14:12

men and women who believe same life-force that worked through Yeshua works through them too. For example:

- Phineas Parkhurst Quimby – an early 19th Century healer in New England who verifiably healed tens of thousands of patients by harnessing their mind power and provided the inspiration for the Christian Science Movement.
- João Teixeira de Faria (a.k.a. John of G_d) - a present day medium and psychic surgeon from Brasil. Millions of people have consulted him since 1965. He claims (like Yeshua) to act as a vehicle for G_d's healing. He says, 'I do not cure anybody. G_d heals. I am merely an instrument in G_d's divine hands'.
- Madre Virginia – a former nun who was thrown out of the Catholic Church for her clairvoyance and healing abilities. She runs the Hôpital do Senhor (Hospital of the Lord) in her home city. I can personal testify to her extraordinary insight and ability to carry out healing at a distance. Like João Teixeira de Faria she takes none of the credit for herself.

116. In 1st Century Palestine, people believed it possible for spiritual forces to influence the physical world

The gospels report a number of miracles in which Yeshua appeared to circumvent the normal laws of nature. His very first miracle, according to the Fourth Gospel (it appears nowhere else), was turning water into wine[178]. The author says he did it to show that he really was the Son of G_d. This flies in the face of Yeshua's stance in the other gospels where he repeatedly warns against expecting miraculous signs. 'An evil and adulterous generation

---

[178] John 2:1-11

asks for a sign,' he says in the Second Gospel[179], 'but no sign will be given except the sign of Jonah[180].' So in the Synoptics he repeatedly instructs those who witness his miracles not to tell anyone.

Three gospel miracles involve boats and water. In the first Yeshua instructs Cephas[181], his leading disciple, to catch a fish from the lake. In its mouth is a coin which he uses to settle his tax account.[182] In the second he is asleep in a boat when a gale strikes up and the boat starts to fill with water. He calms the storm and then demands of his disciples why they had so little faith.[183] Third, in 'Mark' and 'John' he walks across the lake to rescue the disciples in a storm.[184] 'Matthew' adds an extra twist to the story: the hapless Cephas tries to walk on the water, but he loses his nerve and begins to sink. Yeshua catches him, saying, 'You of little faith, why did you doubt?' [185]All three of these stories are quite clearly allegories for the power of faith.

Another miracle was the feeding of the five (or was it four) thousand.[186] All four gospels report that Yeshua took a small quantity of food and fed a hungry crowd. The implication is that he somehow multiplied some loaves and fishes so that all ate and were filled. There were even many baskets of food left over (but the authors don't say where the baskets came from!).

---

179   Matthew 16:4
180   Scholars believe this is a cross-reference between Jonah coming back after three days inside the whale and Jesus' resurrection from the dead after three days.
181   a.k.a. Peter or Simon Peter
182   Matthew 17:24-27
183   Luke 8:22-25
184   Mark 6:45-52, John 6:16-21
185   Matthew 14:22-33
186   E.g. Mark 6:30-44 and Mark 8:1-9

Are we supposed to believe that these miracles really happened? In 1st Century Palestine, most people believed in miracles. They believed it possible for spiritual forces to influence the physical world, and that some people could control those forces. Some still do – for instance, the people who flock to Lourdes looking for a cure. But to most 21st Century audiences, the miracle stories are superstitious and primitive. Any modern, rational, educated person is bound to question whether they really happened in the way they are described.

It all comes down to the thorny question of belief. Those who believe that Yeshua was who the church says he was would, of course, say 'yes', they really happened. They believe it so it's true. For them Yeshua really did walk on water and bring Lazarus's rotting corpse back to life. But they're flying in the face of the evidence. Yeshua was human, and humans simply don't walk on water unaided. Try it! And despite the medical advances of the past few decades, once a body has started to rot, that's it, it's over.

The gospel authors saw Yeshua as a miracle worker, and they wanted their readers to think of him this way too. Did Yeshua's late 1st Century followers think the miracle stories proved he was Son of G_d? Probably. But half a century earlier even the disciples who supposedly witnessed the miracles were generally so unimpressed that when Yeshua was arrested they fled back to Galilee!

117. A miracle is any event that cannot be explained by the known laws of science and nature

A miracle is any event in the physical world that cannot be explained by the known laws of science and nature. These change as scientific knowledge advances. In times gone by – mobile phones, fast cars, television, the internet etc. would have been considered miracles. Even flicking a switch to light up a room would have appeared miraculous to the average person a century and a half ago, and in some parts of the world it still would.

The laws of physics have not changed in the past two thousand years; indeed, they have never changed, not in two thousand *billion* years! But our knowledge of them has. Every major scientific advance makes a 'miracle' no longer a miracle. Today space flight is no miracle, but transporting ourselves across space instantaneously as they do in certain science fiction programmes (such as Star Trek) would be. But for now, we can't, so it appears just as miraculous as a pistol shot would have done five hundred years ago.

As for the healing miracles, if they happened (and I genuinely believe some of them did) who's to say they weren't the placebo effect at work? Scientists have demonstrated that placebos - pills with no active ingredients - can produce miraculous cures when the patient believes they can, and the stronger the belief, the more effective the cure. It's perfectly possible that people who believed in Yeshua's power to heal would get better simply for that reason.

Perhaps the gospel authors saw no harm in massaging the facts to fit their stories – perhaps they even believed them themselves. But there are no historical references to Yeshua transcending the laws of nature outside the New Testament other than as one of several gifted healers. Don't you think there would be if something as remarkable as bringing a dead body back to life or turning water into wine had taken place? These two events didn't even make it into the other three gospels!

118. Yeshua sometimes took deliberate action to make a point

The gospels give many examples of Yeshua taking deliberate action to make a point. The best known is the carefully planned demonstration staged in the holiest of Jewish holy places when he drove the market traders and money changers from the courtyard of the Jerusalem Temple[187]. This was a direct challenge to the Temple authorities and also the Romans, who had no interest in Jewish religious disputes, but every interest in maintaining law and order. Yeshua was lucky not to be arrested immediately for disturbing the peace.

In the Synoptics this incident takes place during the last week of his life; the Fourth Gospel reports this incident at the start of his ministry. Which is it? They can't both be right! Some gospel apologists attempt to paper over the cracks by suggesting it happened twice, but if this were true it would surely have hastened his end.

Another example comes from the Fourth Gospel[188]. During the Last Supper, Yeshua washes his disciples' feet. Cephas objects, which gives the author the opportunity to place a long speech on service and humility in Yeshua's mouth. There is no mention of this in the other gospels.

---

[187] Zechariah 14:21 prophesied: 'And there shall no longer be traders in the house of the Lord of hosts on that day.'

[188] John 13:5-20

ARREST AND TRIAL

119. The gospels don't explain why Yeshua was in terror if he was certain he would rise again

The gospels say that Yeshua spent the last week of his life in Jerusalem baiting the religious leaders with provocative teachings and incisive retorts. By the end of that week the Jewish authorities wanted him dead, but they knew he was popular with the people and if they arrested him in the city during the day a riot would break out. They would have to seize him at night, if they could find him.

Yeshua retired to the Garden of Gethsemane on the edge of the city after the Last Supper, agitated and distressed. The Third Gospel says he sweated blood[189]. All four had said that he predicted exactly what was going to happen, that he would be arrested, handed over, mocked and killed, and that he would rise again after three days[190]. But they don't explain why Yeshua was in such terror if he was certain he would rise again. 'Luke' says the disciples fell asleep[191] then an angel appeared and gave Yeshua strength (remember, 'Luke' was fond of angels). Then he woke up the disciples and the temple guard appeared to arrest him, led by the treacherous Judas Iscariot. The eleven remaining disciples fled and his trusted lieutenant, Cephas, later denied he knew

---

[189] Luke 22: 42-44

[190] E.g. Mark 10:34

[191] There's an amusing lyric in Andrew Lloyd Webber and Tim Rice's 'Jesus Christ Superstar' in which the drunken disciples in the Garden of Gethsemane are looking forward to retiring and writing the gospels so people will still talk about them when they die!

him. They were in a state of fear and with every reason: soon they could be rounded up by the Romans and made to suffer the same fate.

120. The gospels differ significantly over Yeshua's trial

The gospels say Yeshua was sent for trial, but the four gospels differ significantly:

- In the First Gospel, they took him to Caiaphas, the high priest's, house where the Sanhedrin, the Jewish governing council had assembled. Caiaphas was effectively the ruler of Judea and it seems he got on well with the Roman Prefect, Pontius Pilate. As long as Caiaphas kept order and taxes were paid, Pilate left him alone. Pilate maintained a small Roman garrison at Caesarea close to Jerusalem on the coast, just in case.

  The Jewish leaders gave false and conflicting testimony; Yeshua remained silent. Then Caiaphas asked him if he was the Messiah. Previously he had refused to claim the title, but this time he answered, 'I am.' 'Blasphemy!' exclaimed the Jewish leaders, 'The punishment is death.' [192] But the Jewish authorities had no power to execute a prisoner, only the Roman Prefect could do that, so Yeshua was sent to Pilate.

  Pilate is said to be unconvinced by the evidence presented to him and told the Sanhedrin to prosecute Yeshua themselves since blasphemy was not his concern. The Jewish leaders then accused Yeshua of claiming to be a king; this could be seen as sedition, a capital offence under Roman law. Still at first Pilate could find no reason to execute him. Finally he caved in, had him flogged and

---

[192]   Mark 14:53 - 15:15

then sent for crucifixion – a sadistic method of execution reserved for bandits, slaves and non-Romans guilty of disloyalty to the Emperor.

- In 'Luke's' Gospel, and only 'Luke's', he was also sent to Herod Antipas, the ruler of Galilee, who questioned him but took no action and returned him to Pilate.
- 'Matthew' added a further dramatic gesture – Pilate washed his hands to signify that he was innocent of Yeshua's blood.
- And typically the Fourth Gospel added several lengthy passages of dialogue at all stages of the proceedings.

121. The gospels do not explain why the Jewish crowd suddenly switched from cheering Yeshua to baying for his blood

The gospels claim that Pilate was in the habit of releasing one prisoner every festival and appealed to the crowd to nominate Yeshua for an amnesty. But they would not, preferring to plead for a common thief, Barabbas, instead. As for Yeshua, they screamed at Pilate to crucify him.

This is curious. No convincing explanation is given for Jewish crowd changing from cheering and waving palm leaves as he entered the city to baying for his blood within a couple of days. Besides, the custom of the Romans releasing a prisoner at the Passover festival is unheard of outside the gospels so we must conclude there was no such custom. And a Roman Governor had absolute discretion. The Pilate of history had a fearsome reputation and would never have allowed the crowd to choose.

122. The Second and Fourth Gospels had every reason to portray 'the Jews' as pleading for Yeshua's death

The authors of the Second and Fourth Gospels had their own reasons to portray 'the Jews' as desperate for Yeshua's death. 'Matthew's' Gospel has the Jewish crowd yelling in unison, 'His blood be on us and on our children!'[193] It is extremely doubtful that this was written by the original author. The Fourth Gospel was so keen to absolve Pilate of his responsibilities that it said he nailed an inscription to the cross in three languages, 'Yeshua of Nazareth, King of the Jews'[194]. The chief priests objected, demanding that 'This man said I am.....' be added to the inscription. But Pilate stood firm, saying, 'What I have written I have written.'

Incidentally, to condemn Yeshua for sedition would have been a major miscarriage of justice since there is no evidence in any of the gospels that Yeshua had political or military aspirations.

123. The real Pilate was a ruthless tyrant, not a kindly ditherer

Few scholars regard the gospel reports of Yeshua's 'trial' as factually credible. The gospels say Yeshua had broken no law in Roman eyes and only when the chief priests convinced Pilate that he was a danger to public order was his fate sealed. But this is extremely unlikely. Roman Prefects could treat members of the subject nation more or less as they wished. Pilate was not the weak and wavering man portrayed in the gospels, but a ruthless tyrant who had no hesitation in putting usurpers to death without trial.

'Matthew' was so keen to absolve the Romans of their responsibility that he has Pilate's wife advising him in to 'have nothing to do

---

[193]   Matthew 27:25
[194]   John 19: 19-22

with this innocent man for today I have suffered a great deal because of a dream about him.'[195]

The gospel authors faced a dilemma – how could they explain why this notoriously stubborn and vindictive man allowed himself to be persuaded to send Yeshua to his death even though he believed that he had no charge to answer. Outside the gospel stories there is no record of Pilate ever showing mercy, and it would have been completely out of character to let Yeshua off the hook.[196] If he posed a threat to law and order his fate would have been quickly sealed.

Pilate's reluctance in the gospels to crucify this noisy Jewish dissident contrasts so much with what is known about him from other sources that it seems certain that later editors 'doctored' the gospels to deflect blame away from Rome.

124. The Christian leaders did not want to make enemies of the Romans

The truth is, Yeshua must have been a political threat to the Roman authorities. He jeopardised the stability of Jerusalem at a sensitive time, so they executed him using the punishment reserved for seditionists - crucifixion. And it is doubtful that Pilate would have lost any sleep over it.

In the decades that followed, the Romans took charge of the religion and put the finishing touches to the Christian Scriptures. The gospels became their apologists. Once Christianity had become the official religion of the empire, it would have been

---

[195] Matthew 27:19. There is no mention of this in the other gospels.
[196] He was later recalled to Rome to face charges of misrule and committed suicide in disgrace, but that had nothing to do with Yeshua.

embarrassing to say the least that a senior Roman official had condemned the Saviour to death! It was convenient to deflect the blame for his death to the Jews. The repercussions for Christian-Jewish relations were severe and lasted for nearly two thousand years, until Pope John Paul the Second made a wholesome apology to the Jewish people for anti-semitism in 2000.[197]

125. The crucifixion is verified by non-gospel sources

After the trial, if indeed one ever took place (which is doubtful), Yeshua was taken out of the city and nailed to a cross. We can rely on the gospels' reports that the crucifixion took place, even if we can't accept all the details, because they are verified by other sources. Besides, no apostle would have made up a story that his Master had suffered a humiliating death normally reserved for insurgents and thieves. And we can be fairly certain at which time of the year the crucifixion took place since the gospels state categorically that it was Passover time, which means in the Spring.

126. The gospels disagree over Yeshua's last words

It was normal for victims to suffer for many hours in the heat of the day, then slip into a coma before being pronounced dead. Usually it took over twenty-four hours to die, but the gospels say Yeshua died relatively quickly. But what were his last words?

- According to 'Matthew' he let out a cry, 'My G_d, my G_d, why have you forsaken me?'[198] – hardly the cry of a man who had participated willingly in his fate.

---

[197] In 2000, Pope John Paul also apologised for the crusades, the massacre of French Protestants and the trial of Galileo.

[198] Matthew 27:46. This is a quote from Psalms 22.1.

- In 'Luke', he cried more nobly, 'Father, into your hands I commend my spirit.'[199]
- In 'Mark', he merely breathed his last.[200] 'Mark' claimed that Pilate was surprised that Yeshua died so soon – as if he cared![201]
- In 'John' he said nothing profound, but took the opportunity to ask 'the disciple who he loved'[202] to take care of his mother.

Interestingly members of the public were not allowed to get close to the crucifixion location so it seems unlikely anyone other than the Roman guards would have heard any words spoken by the condemned.

127. The circumstances of Yeshua's burial are hotly debated

While Yeshua's crucifixion is not in doubt, the circumstances of his burial are vigorously contested.

It was unheard of for a crucified person to receive a decent burial; this was part of the punishment. It was normal practice to leave crucified bodies on the crosses until the vultures had torn off the flesh, then remove the bones and take them to the sulphur pits outside Jerusalem which were used as a crematorium. Alternatively the naked body would be left on the cross so that vultures could attack, which was considered an excellent deterrent

---

[199] Luke 23, 46
[200] Mark 15:37
[201] Mark 15:44
[202] There are several references to 'the disciple who Yeshua loved' in the Fourth Gospel. Those who think it was the gospel author himself are mistaken for the reasons already cited.

to other would-be insurrectionists. Any remains would then be placed in a shallow grave or eaten by dogs.

To say this, of course, would not have suited the gospel writers. Instead they wrote that Pilate gave permission for Yeshua's body to be taken by an influential admirer, Joseph of Arimithea, and placed in a tomb that he had constructed for himself. With Mary Magdalene and another Mary looking on, a large stone was rolled across the entrance and an armed guard positioned close by.

Quite why Pilate would have given permission for the body of this particular troublemaker to be given this special treatment is unclear, except it set the scene for what followed next.

RESURRECTION?

128. Nobody saw Yeshua walk out of the tomb

Before a murder charge can be proven, lawyers demand to know what happened to the body. In Yeshua's case, the only honest answer would have to be, 'We don't know.' Nobody saw him walk out of the tomb. Was the body actually taken there? Again, nobody knows, but the balance of probability (taking account everything we know about crucifixion in those times) is that Yeshua's body ended up where all crucifixion victims did – either in a sulphur pit or as the vultures' or dogs' dinner. Harsh – but almost certainly true.

Why lie? When Yeshua died, his disciples were scared and confused. Their hopes that he was the one to liberate his people were shattered. Then, as the decades rolled by, successive generations of Christians began to see him as the personification of G_d. But how could G_d die? How could they execute G_d as a common criminal? Why didn't he try to escape? Paul of Tarsus, the gospel writers, letter writers and subsequent theologians had a lot of explaining to do! The explanation they came up with was startling – resurrection.

129. Not even his close disciples expected Yeshua to rise again

According to the gospels, Yeshua repeatedly told his disciples that he would be killed and then resurrected on the third day[203]; this was his destiny as foretold in the Hebrew Scriptures. And yet

---

[203] E.g. Mark 9:31 and 10:34; Matthew 16:21 and 17:23; Luke 9:22 and 24:7; John 20:19

according to these same sources, nobody – not even his closest disciples – expected him to rise again. When the post-Easter Christ figure 'appeared' to them, all the witnesses were surprised, so much so that most did not recognise him. How could this be? Had they forgotten his words? Did they misunderstand them? Why did it come as such a surprise when it (allegedly) happened? Or were the living Yeshua's claims that he would come back to life an invention of the gospel authors?

Bishop Jenkins, already referred to for his comments on the immaculate conception (page 84), attracted even more publicity by saying it was not necessary for a Christian to believe in a physical resurrection. He described it as a 'conjuring trick with bones'. This caused such uproar there was talk of bringing back heresy trials. Although no-one suggested he should be burnt at the stake, several commentators insisted that his views on Christianity should be thoroughly discounted since he didn't subscribe to standard doctrine.

In retirement this enlightened man called for the abolition of the Church of England, which he described as a medieval institution which no longer has any relevance. In response, a fellow bishop politely suggested his former colleague had gone senile!

130. Paul of Tarsus believed that Yeshua returned in changed form, not as a resuscitated corpse

The earliest reference to a resurrection appears in Paul's First Letter to the Corinthians, dating from around a quarter of a century after the crucifixion. Paul never claimed a *physical* resurrection; he believed that Yeshua had reappeared in *changed* form; not a resuscitated corpse but transformed into a spiritual body. Perhaps that's why he was not easily recognized by his followers.

Paul claimed to have seen a vision of the risen Christ himself and knew of many other instances. He wrote, 'For I handed on to you as of first important what I in turn had received,' including a number of 'appearances' to the twelve disciples (strange – after Judas's suicide there were only supposed to be eleven) and to a much larger group of believers.[204]

The writers of the Second, Third and Fourth Gospels did not agree. They went to some lengths to insist that the risen Yeshua was not a ghost, nor was he a badly injured man hobbling around. Even though he could appear and disappear at will, he ate, drank and could be touched.

131. The Synoptic Gospels accounts of the Easter story are totally inconsistent

Between them the gospels report dozens of sightings of the risen Yeshua. Most began and ended mysteriously. Usually he 'drew near' then 'disappeared from sight'.

- The First Gospel ended with the body missing and an angel telling the astonished disciples to return to Galilee where they would see him. They were clearly not expecting this, and fled in terror.[205] Decades later, twelve extra verses were added in which the Christ figure 'appeared' to them several times. He spoke to them and was immediately whisked away to heaven (contradicting the Ascension account in the opening chapter of Acts of the Apostles). The New Revised Standard Version of the New Testament says in the footnotes that some authorities mark these verses 'doubtful'. Nowhere does either the

---

[204] 1 Corinthians: 3–8
[205] Mark 16: 5–8

original author or the later contributor claim that Yeshua had risen in bodily form.

- In the Second Gospel, Mary Magdalene and another Mary encountered Yeshua as they fled from the empty tomb, but they didn't recognize him. Clearly he wasn't the man they remembered from just a few days earlier. He told them to instruct the disciples to return to Galilee where they would see him and several sightings are reported. The writer adds an interesting postscript: the Jewish leaders, petrified of what would happen if the word got out that Yeshua had come back to life, paid the soldiers guarding the tomb to spread the story that the disciples came by night and stole the body while they were asleep. 'This story is still told among the Jews to this day,' he wrote.[206]

- The Third Gospel added several more appearances in which Yeshua 'came near' and 'stood among them', showed them his wounds, ate fish, then vanished. There are no such claims in 'Mark' or 'Matthew'. Later, he 'withdrew from them and was carried up to heaven.'[207] All of this happened on the third day, Easter Sunday. None of these stories concurred with the other gospels. Moreover, far from fleeing to Galilee, the disciples stayed in Jerusalem and 'were continually in the temple.'

- In the Fourth Gospel, Mary Magdalene discovered the empty tomb and went to fetch Cephas and 'the disciple who Yeshua loved.'[208] They ran back to the tomb, then the two disciples 'returned to their homes.' (It's not clear where these 'homes' were. It's implausible that they had homes in Jerusalem). Mary then encountered two angels by the tomb who told her Yeshua had risen. She turned

---

[206] Matthew 28:15
[207] Luke 24:50-51
[208] John 20:2

round and he was standing behind her, but she did not recognise him. He told her not to touch him because he had not yet 'ascended to the Father.'[209] She then reported back to the disciples.

Later, says 'John', he 'stood among' the disciples and invited 'doubting' Thomas to touch his wounds.[210] He also he appeared to the disciples on various occasions, once while they ate bread and fish for breakfast and one in which he appeared on a beach and gave the disciples some advice on fishing.[211] It seems highly likely that these episodes were written specifically to convince the faithful that Yeshua's actual physical body had come back to life.

• Acts of the Apostles, written by the same author as the Third Gospel, merely says he 'presented himself alive' to the disciples over a *forty day period* before the momentous events of Pentecost.

Once again we find ourselves wondering which, if any, of these accounts is correct, since they can't all be right!

There seems little doubt that some of Yeshua's followers felt the presence of their Master after his death and others thought they saw visions. We must not be too sceptical about this. It's not unusual for bereaved people today to 'see' a departed loved one or imagine they are around them. Their experiences, whatever they were, must have felt very real, because many of them later suffered and died for their faith.

But surely if a body had come back to life in a physical sense it would have been reported in the historical records of the day, not

---

[209] John 20:17

[210] John 20:19-20

[211] John 21:4-6

only in the devotional literature (the gospels). Then the whole of the known world would have been won over.

132. The only things the gospels agree on is that the tomb was empty on the third day and Mary Magdalene was one of those who discovered it

The gospel writers had a difficult task on their hands: explaining a situation for which there was no logical explanation – an empty tomb. Taking all the gospels together, the only things they agree on is that the tomb was empty on the third day and Mary Magdalene was one of those who discovered that this was so. None of the gospels explain how Yeshua was encountered in the garden fully clothed, considering the burial clothes were left in situ.

The church likes to sweep aside the differences as if they don't matter, but they do because they cast doubt on the accuracy of all four versions. The authors were so keen to persuade their readers that Yeshua had risen from the dead they overlooked important details. Many explanations have been given, some more plausible than others:

- All these stories are concoctions.
- The body was never taken there in the first place.
- It was stolen as 'Matthew' suggested.
- He was taken down from the cross still alive.
- He was drugged by some herbal potion.
- The witnesses hallucinated.
- The disciples lied.
- The women lied.
- The gospel writers were misled.

- The gospel writers lied.
- Later editors changed the facts to fit the story.

... and so on. You, the reader, must decide. But bear in mind that with many of the gospel stories, the longer the period between Yeshua's life (c 5 BCE-30 CE) and the writing of the gospel (c 70 CE – 105 CE), the more embellished they become.

133. The risen Yeshua appeared only to believers

One of the keys to understanding what really happened is this: the gospels state that the risen Yeshua appeared only to believers. Why, if the Jewish people as a whole – or both Jews and gentiles - were his intended audience? Psychologists tell us that we are just as likely to see what we believe as believe what we see, in other words, our beliefs colour our perceptions. May we conclude that there's no verifiable evidence for a physical resurrection, just the words of a handful of devoted authors keen to show that Yeshua was not defeated by the Romans, and that G-d vindicated him even though his chosen people had not recognised him as the Messiah?

It seems surprising to non-Christians that otherwise reasonable people in the 21st century should so readily believe tales such as these, but we should remember that closed communities tend to conform to the prevailing beliefs of the group, whether Christians, Scientologists, Muslims or Jehovah's Witnesses etc.

Of course, the resurrection cannot be verified. You either believe that the gospel writers knew the truth and told nothing but the truth, or you don't. (If you do believe, you still have to explain which of the four conflicting versions you believe.) The early Christians believed it, and it became the foundation stone of the

Christian religion. Regardless of the facts, whatever you decide to believe is true – for you. That's the way the human mind works.

134. Easter is far more important than Christmas in the Christian calendar

Today, Easter is unquestionably the most important day of the Christian calendar, although Christmas is celebrated more enthusiastically.

Easter Sunday is the day on which Christians celebrate Yeshua's coming back to life and was seen in corporeal form for several weeks before ascending on a cloud to 'heaven'. This is the very basis of their religion. They believe it because the gospels say it happened, *or so they think*. As we've seen, the gospels are far from clear on the nature of the 'resurrection' or the timing of the 'Ascension', but most Christians aren't aware of the inconsistencies in the scriptures.

The Easter stories transformed Yeshua's abject shame and defeat into a noble sacrifice, the triumph of life over death, victory over the Romans and his ultimate vindication before G_d. Easter became the crux of traditional Christianity and the cross its most widely recognised symbol.

135. The earliest reference to the sign of the cross dates from around 200 CE

The cross (or crucifix) has become the main symbol of Christianity, seen in churches, homes and public places and often worn as a brooch or on a chain around the neck. In churches it is often shown on a portrait or statue showing a contorted Yeshua in agony, festooned with thorns and dripping with blood.[212] At Easter time, wooden crosses are carried through the streets in many countries.

The earliest Christian art (dating from the 1st Century) doesn't show the sign of the cross. It was considered shameful since crucifixion was reserved for the lowest criminals. The first reference to Christians using the cross as a symbol date from around 200 CE when Christians in North Africa traced the sign of the cross across their foreheads. Nowadays it is usually made across the abdomen as a form of blessing or protection for oneself.

The use of the crucifix as a symbol owes much to Paul of Tarsus. He wrote, 'For the message of the cross is foolishness to those who are perishing, but to us who are being saved it is the power of G_d;' and, 'May I never boast of anything except the cross of our Lord Jesus Christ, by which the world has been crucified to me, and I to the world.'[213]

---

[212] Personally I would prefer to see the benign image of the statue of which looks down lovingly at the world from the top of Corcovado Mountain in Rio de Janeiro as the universal symbol of Christ the Redeemer.

[213] 1 Corinthians, 1:18 and Galatians 6:14

ASCENSION AND PENTECOST

136. In 1st Century Palestine the Earth was believed to be flat, heaven was above the clouds and hell below ground.

In 1st Century Palestine (and throughout the Western World at that time), the Earth was believed to be flat. Heaven, where G_d lived, was above the clouds and hell below ground. Christians, of course, decry Hades, the underworld where the dead go in Greek mythology, and take hell seriously. But what's the difference?

When two of the gospels, 'Mark' and 'Luke', said that the risen Master was carried up to heaven and placed at the right hand of G_d,[214] this would have accorded with the worldview of their readers, as would Acts stating that the disciples watched as he was 'lifted up, and a cloud took him out of their sight.'[215] (The other two gospels have nothing to say on the subject.) Neither author said any more about the cloud, and probably nobody asked.

We've seen (many times) that there's nothing unusual about the books of the New Testament contradicting *each other*, but here the *same author*, the man who wrote both 'Luke' and Acts, contradicts *himself*. In 'Luke's Gospel' he says the Ascension happened soon after the post-resurrection appearances, probably the same day; in Acts he says the Christ figure appeared for forty days before a cloud took him away.

Of course, very few people still believe in a three-storey world with a heaven above. The prospect of a man being physically lifted

---

[214] Mark 16:19 (in the coda); Luke 24:51
[215] Acts 1:9

up into the sky on a cloud is, of course, ludicrous to a 21ˢᵗ Century audience now we know that the Earth is a globe and there's only space above the clouds, but, if you are to take Christianity literally, this is precisely what you are supposed to believe. And incredibly there are still people who believe this!

137. How Yeshua will return is never explained

The early Christians believed that Yeshua would soon return to Earth to establish the Kingdom of G_d and save those who believed in him from eternal annihilation.

Many modern day Christians still believe he will return and it is regularly expounded from church pulpits on Sundays. Most do not specify a timescale, and most do not feel the need to explain why it has not yet happened despite the Synoptic Gospel writers' insistence that it would happen in their own time. Nor do they explain just how Yeshua will return. If he really is 'up there' somewhere, can we expect him to float down on a cloud or descend strapped to a parachute, or what? If so it will be worth seeing!

138. Acts of the Apostles begins with the events of Pentecost

The gospel stories end with Yeshua's ascension; 'Acts of the Apostles' begins with the events of Pentecost. At Pentecost the disciples were gathered in Jerusalem when a sound came from heaven, tongues of fire rested on each of them and they were filled with the 'Holy Spirit'. They began to speak in other languages and onlookers thought they were drunk. Cephas then delivers a speech *aimed only at Jews* announcing Yeshua as the Messiah and urging them to repent and be baptised.

Thus began a chapter in the life of the early church in which the disciples (now called 'apostles') travelled widely spreading their message, not always to receptive audiences. Resistance among Jews who did not regard Yeshua as the Messiah grew. From 100 CE onwards there were reports of riots among unreceptive Romans and Jews. Some died horrible deaths; some were executed. But somehow the religion spread, and much of the credit is due to the tentmaker, mystic, man of letters, former Pharisee and religious fanatic, Paul of Tarsus.

THE EARLY CHURCH

139. Immediately after Yeshua's death, few believed in him as G_d's messenger

There is no concrete evidence that Yeshua's was seen as G_d's unique messenger around the time of his death, let alone the Messiah or Son of G_d. But beliefs about him were not static; from being an erudite holy man with a gift for healing and an eschatological outlook, beliefs about him continued to evolve. Christians began to experience him in a new way. As the 1st Century CE progressed, his small band of followers came to believe that he was more than just a great prophet and teacher, but the very incarnation of G_d. By the time the Fourth Gospel was written he was no longer seen as a person of flesh and blood, but a supernatural being free of restrictions in time and space. In other words, he *was* G_d.

140. Paul's emergence as an apostle struck a note of discord into the Christian community

Paul's emergence as an apostle from the mid-30s onwards immediately struck a note of discord into the fledgling Christian community. Acts tells us he visited Yeshua's chief disciple Cephas and James (Tiago), Yeshua's biological brother and until his execution in 62 CE[216], the recognised leader of the small Christian group in Jerusalem. There's no record of whether Paul learned anything about Yeshua's life and teachings, but plenty of evidence that he and the other two apostles didn't see eye to eye[217].

Having known Yeshua when he was alive, Cephas and Tiago resented this newcomer taking over their pitch, but Paul was undeterred. He believed Yeshua himself had given him authority to preach in a revelation and was just as qualified as they. In his letter to the Galatians he even berated them for cowardice, inconsistency and hypocrisy.

The main bone of contention was whether the new religion based on Yeshua's activities was open to all or intended solely for Jews. Cephas and Tiago thought it was just for Jews; Paul disagreed. In the long term, Paul's view prevailed. The vast majority of Jews rejected Yeshua as their Messiah and Christianity became a gentile religion. Curiously, though, it was Cephas, not Paul, who was subsequently venerated by the church. Catholics to this day believe that St Peter's Basilica in Rome was built above Cephas's grave, although there's no conclusive evidence he was buried there[218].

---

[216] Reported by Josephus.

[217] Galatians 2:7-8

[218] As recently as November 2013, Pope Francis showed bone fragments he claimed belonged to the Apostle Cephas during an open air mass in St Peter's Square in Rome. The bones were discovered during the excavation of tombs under St Peter's Basilica in the 1940s. The Church has long been undecided on whether the bones are truly those of Cephas, although in 1968 Pope Paul VI claimed that they had been 'identified in a way we can hold to be convincing'. Archaeologists involved in the dig, though, remained unconvinced.

141. Early Christians struggled to work out what their beliefs were and how they should be proclaimed

The first People of the Way were not Christians, but Jews. The early church was rather like the networks of 'house churches' seen in some countries today. It was remarkably informal and egalitarian, and women played a full part. There were no priests, and anyone could speak when they felt moved to do so. They set high standards of behaviour for themselves. For example, urged on by Paul of Tarsus, they were more rigorous about sexual behaviour than the communities around them and celibacy became prized.

Theirs was not a happy community, and there was much infighting. There were deep divisions over what to believe, for instance, over who Yeshua was and the relevance of the Hebrew traditions. Soon after Yeshua's death, the community began to tear themselves apart over whether his teachings were for everyone or just for his own people, the Jews. This remained unresolved for several decades.

Two main parallel movements emerged. On the one hand, Yeshua's earthly disciples, led by the Apostle Cephas, believed that the new sect must stay firmly within the Jewish tradition (although he later softened on this). They argued that Christian converts must first convert to Judaism, which meant observing the food laws and, for men, the agony of circumcision.

Paul strongly disagreed. He rejected Jewish Law and declared that Yeshua's message was for all. For him the death and resurrection of Yeshua (in a transformed, spiritual body, remember) had made the 613 strictures of the Torah redundant. No longer did he believe that doing good works was the way to salvation; what mattered was having faith in the resurrection, which signalled the imminent coming of the Kingdom of G_d and was the sure road to redemption. He took his message all over the Eastern Mediterranean, believing that he had been personally called to take the good news to the gentiles.

The two sides could not appeal to the gospels because they had not yet been written, but they would not have helped because they are far from clear. Generally they present Yeshua as a man largely content to preach to his own people although he did not dismiss anyone who came to him for help, including a Roman Centurion and a Samaritan woman. But there's no disguising the fact that the gospels do not agree. For example, 'Matthew' has Yeshua telling the disciples to spread the word but not to the gentiles or Samaritans[219]. 'Luke' announces the coming of Yeshua, the Messiah child, as a 'light to the gentiles' as well as bringing glory to Israel,[220] and even cites a Samaritan as being more worthy than a Jewish priest in the Parable of the Good Samaritan[221]. The Fourth Gospel, written at a time when Christianity had separated from Judaism and relationships between Christians and Jews had turned sour, asserts that Yeshua treated people from non-Jewish backgrounds as equals.

Meanwhile, the Gnostics took an entirely different view. As we've seen, Gnostics believed that G_d must be found through knowledge of truth and practising what one knows rather than faith in Yeshua. For them he was primarily a great teacher, the 'pathfinder'. In later decades they were roundly denounced by the fledgling Roman Church. Indeed, many theologians declared heretical by the early church make perfect sense today. Origen (185-254 CE) is a case in point. He said a human being is flesh,

---

[219]   Matthew 10:5

[220]   Luke 2:32

[221]   Luke 10:29-37

corruptible and corrupted; spirit; and soul, the highest part. He taught that G_d could be reached through direct experience and salvation could be realised through human effort. But his voice was drowned out a century and a half later by the towering figure of the theologian Bishop Augustine of Hippo (354-430 CE – more of him later).

142. Persecution of Christians started in the seventh decade of the 1st Century

Persecution of Christians started in the Emperor Nero's time. In 64 CE, about the time Paul of Tarsus was detained in Rome, a fire destroyed half of the city. Nero blamed the 'followers of Chrestus', claiming they'd brought a curse on the city because they wouldn't worship the Roman gods. They were considered be to superstitious eccentrics with crazy beliefs. Many were tortured and killed. They were frequently attacked and served up as entertainment in Roman arenas. Despite this, numbers continued to grow.

The early Christians did not make themselves popular. They regarded all other religions as false and even demonic (many Christians still do). They annoyed Jews and Romans alike with their secrecy and superior attitude. Moreover, their loyalty to Rome was constantly questioned. They had to keep on the move and often had to escape under cover of darkness. By the 2nd Century it had become a glorious thing for Christians to die a painful death with dignity rather than deny their religion. It was the road to eternal life, and an honour to emulate the sufferings of their saviour.

The Romans only stopped persecuting Christians in 313 CE after two hundred years of ridicule and contempt. This followed the Milan Edict, an order from the Emperor Constantine, a crucial episode in the history of Christianity (more of this later).

143. If the Romans had not sacked the city in 70 CE, Jerusalem would have become the centre of Christianity

In 70 CE the Christian community in Jerusalem, by then a couple of thousand strong, was scattered when the city was ransacked by the Romans. This marked a watershed and undoubtedly had an enormous effect on the writers of the Synoptic Gospels. The First was written about this time and the Second and Third a few years after. In all three Yeshua appears to have forecast this event, but whether he actually did or not no-one knows for sure. The authors probably hoped that he would return to save the city.

Perhaps if this had not happened Jerusalem, not Rome, would have become the centre of Christianity; it would have been the logical choice, but Rome became pre-eminent since it was the undisputed centre of imperial power and the two leading apostles, Cephas and Paul, were supposedly buried there. There is little doubt that Rome was Paul's final resting place but we can't be sure about Cephas; scholars suspect that his martyrdom in Rome is a fiction created to give him equal status with Paul and establish the line of popes. St Peter's Basilica was built above the place where he was reported to be buried.

144. Cephas's early successors as Bishop of Rome are probably just names

By 200 CE there was a Catholic Church centred on Rome, with a pope, clergy and bishops. Catholics believe that that the current pope is the latest in a continuous succession dating right back to Cephas, but this is extremely doubtful.

Professor Diarmaid MacCulloch offers his expert view in his book, *A History of Christianity*: 'Cephas's early successors as Bishop of Rome are probably just names, probably an attempt to create a history of succession.' There is no reliable evidence of a continuous succession of popes starting with the Apostle Cephas.[222]

---

[222] Of course Yeshua was avidly opposed to the 'popes' and 'bishops' of his own religion – the Sadducees, Chief Priest, Temple Priests and scribes. Anyone seeing sartorially lavish processions of churchmen and women that accompany the big national occasions can surely envisage the Chief Priests and scribes of Yeshua's day parading with pride before their people.

THE ROMAN TAKEOVER AND BEYOND

145. Christianity would probably have disappeared had not the Emperor Constantine converted in the early years of the 4th Century

One of the great puzzles about the Christian religion is how a small group of people, inspired by a man who left no writings, made little impression during his lifetime, held no important office and died a criminal's death at a relatively young age, went on to have such a major influence on the world. Believers of course say it is because this man was G_d in human form sent to Earth to redeem humanity and his enduring influence is simply because the stories written about him are true.

Historians have a quite different explanation. They point out that Christianity would probably have disappeared or squabbled itself into obscurity had not the Emperor Constantine converted in the early years of the 4th Century. Without this the fledgling religion would probably have remained a small sect or faded away, as relevant today as Zeus, Jupiter, Odin or Baal. In 313 CE, Constantine issued the 'Edict of Milan' which guaranteed full religious freedom to the Christians, setting them on a par with other religions. It marked the end of official persecution of Christians and put an end to the first age of martyrs.

Constantine's conversion followed a dramatic event in 312 CE at the Battle of the Milvian Bridge. He is said to have looked up to the sun before the battle and seen a cross of light above it with the words 'in this sign, you will conquer' in Greek. Constantine ordered his troops to decorate their shields with a Christian symbol, and subsequently they were victorious. Constantine's conversion owed much to superstition and expediency. Even so, within a quarter of a century Christianity had spread throughout the Roman Empire, helped by the heavy hand of Roman military might, and beyond. By the end of the 4th Century, it had become the only official religion of the Empire.

To this day the mainstream churches maintain the alignment between Christianity and the secular authorities worked out at that time. Meanwhile, some nonconformist 'free' churches have long regarded Constantine's adoption of the religion as little short of the fall of 'true' Christianity.

146. The Romans formalised the scriptures, laid down the creeds, strengthened the church hierarchy and increased the power of the papacy

Having adopted it, the Romans set the pattern for the future. They took it upon themselves to decide what the religion stood for and expand on New Testament theology. The term 'Christian' was formally adopted. It had not been widely used at first, although coined by an unknown believer around 47 CE. The word only appears three times in the New Testament, in Acts and in the First Letter of Cephas[223].

The Roman Church formalised the scriptures, laid down the official creeds, strengthened the church hierarchy and increased the power of the papacy. These still heavily influence the Christian religion today.

---

[223] Acts 11:26 and 26:28; 1 Cephas 4:16.

147. The First Council of Nicaea followed the Edict of Milan

The First Council of Nicaea followed soon after the Edict of Milan. Held in 325 CE, it was a defining moment in Christianity. Around three hundred bishops and theologians attended, presided over by the Emperor Constantine himself. Its aim was to iron out disagreements over doctrine. As intended, it effectively placed a straightjacket on the religion.[224]

Among the outcomes of the First Council of Nicaea were three that continue to resonate today: the date of the Easter celebrations (in the Roman world, the first full moon after the Spring Equinox, March 21[225]); the Nicene Creed; and the doctrine of the Holy Trinity.

148. The Nicene Creed prescribed what people should believe

The Nicene Creed was the first statement of official Christian doctrine. It was intended to dictate what the people should believe, create unity and be easy memorised. Remember, the majority of Roman subjects had not chosen Christianity for themselves but been ordered to follow it.

The Nicene Creed is still recited in church today. The wording differs slightly from denomination to denomination, but the following text would be recognised by them all.

---

[224] Professor Diarmaid MacCulloch comments, 'Western theology has been characterised by a tidy-mindedness which reflects the bureaucratic precision of the Latin language, not always to the benefit of its spirituality.' (A History of Christianity, p329).

[225] And so it has been in the Western churches ever since. In the Eastern Orthodox churches it is usually slightly later.

The Nicene Creed

We believe in one God, the Father Almighty, the maker of heaven and earth, of things visible and invisible.

And in one Lord Jesus Christ, the Son of God, the begotten of God the Father, the Only-begotten, that is of the essence of the Father, God of God, Light of Light, true God of true God, begotten and not made; of the very same nature of the Father, by Whom all things came into being, in heaven and on earth, visible and invisible.

Who for us humanity and for our salvation came down from heaven, was incarnate, was made human, was born perfectly of the holy Virgin Mary by the Holy Spirit.

By whom He took body, soul, and mind, and everything that is in man, truly and not in semblance.

He suffered, was crucified, was buried, rose again on the third day, ascended into heaven with the same body, [and] sat at the right hand of the Father.

He is to come with the same body and with the glory of the Father, to judge the living and the dead; of His kingdom there is no end.

We believe in the Holy Spirit, in the uncreated and the perfect; who spoke through the Law, prophets, and Gospels; Who came down upon the Jordan, preached through the apostles, and lived in the saints.

We believe also in only One, Universal, Apostolic, and Holy Church; in one baptism in repentance, for the remission, and forgiveness of sins; and in the resurrection of the dead, in the everlasting judgement of souls and bodies, and the kingdom of Heaven and in the everlasting life.

Source: Wikipedia

149. Not all Christian denominations affirm the Holy Trinity

Nowadays most Christian denominations (the Unitarians being a notable exception) teach that the essence of G_d exists in three forms, the Father, Son and Holy Spirit:

- The Father is as described in the Hebrew Scriptures – creator, Lord, friend and judge.
- The Son, Yeshua, was sent to Earth in human form to redeem humanity; and
- The Holy Spirit is the means by which G_d works on Earth, bringing comfort, life and power.

Christians are urged to worship the Father, follow the example of the Son and live knowing that the Holy Spirit is present within them.

The doctrine of the Holy Trinity was not taught in the 1st Century, it was a later theological invention. The first recorded use of the phrase 'Father, Son and Holy Spirit' in Christian theology is dated as late as 170 CE. The Nicene Creed ingrained it into the minds of the faithful so much so that Yeshua the Son, one third of the Trinity, became part of the popular image of him. But it was certainly not the case during his lifetime.

The Trinity claims scriptural authority from two passages:

- The penultimate verse of the Second Gospel: 'Go therefore and make disciples of all nations, baptizing them in the name of the Father and of the Son and of the Holy Spirit.'[226] However, there is considerable doubt that Yeshua actually said these words or that the original author of the Second Gospel wrote them. Linguistic evidence suggests

---

[226] Matthew 28:19

it was added retrospectively with the specific purpose of justifying the doctrine.

- There's another reference to three 'persons' is in the concluding verse of Paul's second letter to the Corinthians, but his wording hardly specifies a doctrine: 'The grace of the Lord Jesus Christ, the love of G_d and the communion of the Holy Spirit be with all of you.'[227]

150. The doctrine of the Trinity grew out of the Arian Controversy

The doctrine of the Holy Trinity grew out of the Arian Controversy of the 3rd and 4th Centuries CE. Arius (c256-336) was a Christian priest in Alexandria, Egypt. He believed that Yeshua the Son was subordinate to the Father as he had been conceived by G_d, and consequently there had been a time when he had not yet existed. His main adversary was another Alexandrian, Athanasius (c296-336). He argued that the Son was of the same substance as the Father and therefore existed with him from the beginning; there had never been a time when he did not exist. The dispute divided the church and Athanasius won an outright victory at Nicaea. Arius was declared a heretic and saw most of his writings destroyed.

In the centuries that followed Muslims completely rejected the Trinity. While recognising Yeshua as an important prophet, they affirm only one G_d, Allah, with the Prophet Muhammad as its messenger, human, not divine.

---

[227] 2 Corinthians 13:14

151. The Holy Trinity eventually led to the 'Great Schism' of 1054

The doctrine of the Trinity eventually led to the split between the Roman and Eastern Orthodox churches in 1054, known as the 'Great Schism', which has still not been resolved. The Orthodox churches, originally centred on Constantinople, have as long a history as the Roman church, but have had far fewer divisions. They have no equivalent to the Reformation and Counter Reformation, and hardly any burnings, drownings or pogroms against Jews, witches or anyone else.

One of the differences between the Western and Eastern traditions of Christianity is the use of icons. The interiors of Eastern Orthodox churches are covered in them and they are displayed in many homes, but they are rarely seen in Western churches. Icons are images of significant religious figures such as the Christ figure, Yeshua's mother, an evangelist, a saint, or of a holy object such as a cross.

The Hebrew Scriptures forbade the making of images (as does Islam), but Christianity has no such qualms. Christians are known to have made created devotional images from the beginning of the 2nd Century, for instance a shepherd, a dove, fish or boat in a storm. Most had pagan origins and were adopted by Christians for their own use. Images purporting to be of Yeshua, his mother, various saints and even G_d are still the norm in most churches.

152. The solution to the Trinity dispute was fudged at Chalcedon in 451 CE

Like Nicaea a century and a quarter earlier, the Council of Chalcedon (451 CE) was a defining moment in church history. It arose out of continuing confusion about the Doctrine of the

Holy Trinity. The major concern was whether the Father, Son and Holy Spirit were equal, or Father and Son were equal and Spirit subordinate, or Father superior to both, or what?

At the centre of the argument was again the nature of Yeshua. Was he human or divine? How could he be both? If he was of one substance with the Father, then how do we explain his human characteristics – his anger, his tears, his need to rest, the pleasure gained from clean feet and soothing ointment on his head. Could a divine being feel pain? And if he were fully human, why did he not sin when he was on earth? Good questions!

Some theologians gave their lives for one side or the other and bishops even went to war over the issue. Under pressure from the Roman authorities, delegates settled on a compromise. Yeshua was both perfectly divine *and* perfectly human at the same time, the 'Union of Two Natures', G_d and Man. And so it has been in the Western tradition ever since. But many Christians still can't reconcile these two natures in a way that makes sense to non-Christians and, more often than not, themselves.

We now know with the benefit of modern science that we're all *physical* (formed out of the waves and particles that make atoms, cells and human tissue) and '*divine*' (spiritual, formed out of and by consciousness) *at the same time*. But this is not what the revered ecclesiastics at Chalcedon had in mind.

153. Bishop Augustine of Hippo is second only to Paul of Tarsus as the shaper of Roman Christianity

Bishop and theologian Augustine[228] of Hippo (354-430 CE) is second only to Paul of Tarsus as the prime shaper of Roman Christianity. The doctrine of 'Original Sin' was also established by him.

Bishop Augustine's theology was based on the story of Adam and Eve in the Book of Genesis and on Paul's letter to the Romans. He interpreted the opening chapters of Genesis as meaning that human beings were sinful in nature and the body, its needs and desires, inherently evil. Sin was passed down to every member of the human race through sexual reproduction, so every child came into the world already damaged beyond repair. Our only hope was to throw ourselves on the mercy[229] of the Lord Jesus Christ and pledge obedience to his church. Otherwise a grim eternity awaited cut off from G_d in the fires of hell.

Ever since Augustine, the church has over-emphasised the perils of sin and the need for divine forgiveness at the expense of Yeshua's teachings on the wisdom, passion and love of G_d. Paul of Tarsus also regarded our sinfulness as so strong that we cannot conquer it through our actions or our will. We need a transcendent force

---

[228] Not to be confused with the Augustine who led a mission to England in the 6th Century on the orders of the pope and became the first Archbishop of Canterbury.

[229] Incidentally, the word 'mercy' appears frequently in the New Testament, such as in 'Matthew's' version of the Sermon on the Mount, 'Blessed are the merciful, for they will receive mercy,' and 'Be merciful just as your Father is merciful.' (Luke 6:36) These are probably mistranslations. 'Mercy' implies that someone who has the power to harm you chooses to forgive instead and we must beg for mercy. Try substituting 'compassion' for 'mercy' to get closer to the original meaning.

from above. He wrote[230], 'I find..... that when I want to do what is good, evil lies close at hand.... Wretched man that I am! Who will rescue me from this body of death?' For him the risen Christ, of course!

Augustine set the pattern for those of later generations who deprived themselves of physical comforts and even beat themselves thinking this would bring them closer to G-d. But that was not Yeshua's teaching. Why would he have bothered to heal people if he had not considered the body important?

The Western churches continue to highlight the gulf between G_d and humanity created by Original Sin. In contrast, the Eastern Orthodox Churches tend to focus on 'theosis' – the notion that humans can rise to deification and achieve union with the divine, a proposition that seems more in line with Yeshua's gospel teachings.

Yeshua, of course, did not teach eternal damnation (according to the Gospels) but salvation, the opportunity for all to participate in the Kingdom of G_d. The threat of eternal damnation originated in a political deal between the Emperor Justinian and the Eastern Church in 543 CE that created an income stream for the church by decreeing that humankind could only access G_d via the official church. Nine anathemas were imposed by Justinian[231] and sanctioned by the Pope. The curses included the denial of a pre-existent soul before birth, thus refuting the doctrine of reincarnation which had been widely accepted at the time of Yeshua.

More than eight hundred years after Bishop Augustine, Thomas Aquinas (c1225-74), author of *Summa Theologiae,* did not believe

---

[230]   Romans 7:21-25

[231]   Justinian is considered a saint amongst Eastern Orthodox Christians.

that humans were incorrigibly corrupted by sin, but could redeem themselves through their own efforts and by faith and grace. Aquinas was probably the third most important theologian in church history. He became an important figure in the Catholic Church but was unable to purge it of Augustine's negative views.

154. The Protestant forefathers Martin Luther and John Calvin believed that humans could be saved only by grace

After studying the Bible, Paul of Tarsus and Bishop Augustine, Martin Luther (1483-1546) became convinced that humans could not be saved from sin by their own efforts (as taught by Thomas Aquinas) but only by laying hold of G_d's grace by personal faith and total surrender to the Son. John Calvin (1509-1564) took it further. Whilst agreeing that humans could be saved only by grace, he set about creating a society in Geneva based on strict Christian principles, behaviours and laws. Thus began the Reformation and founding of the Protestant Movement.

Protestantism sought to abolish all the mediating entities of medieval Roman Christianity – saints, Maryām the mother of God, priests, icons and relics etc. It also restored the authority of the Bible over the church, its sacraments and clergy. It was therefore desirable for people to be able to read the Bible in their own languages.

155. Translating the Bible was once seen as a grave sin

Until the invention of the printing press, most Christians did not read the Bible. Hand written copies were all that were available and besides they were illiterate. They had to rely on priests to interpret it for them, but in church it was only read in Latin, which most congregations could not understand. It was a serious offence to enable Christians to read the scriptures in their own language, subject to heavy penalties including a long, slow agonising death.

The first hand-written English Bibles predated Luther and Calvin by nearly two hundred years. They were produced in the 1380's by an Oxford Professor, John Wycliffe (1320 – 1384). He and his assistants produced dozens of copies translated out of the Latin Vulgate, the only source text available to them. The church was incensed. One Pope was so infuriated that 44 years after Wycliffe had died he ordered his bones to be dug-up, crushed, and scattered in the river! Previously one of Wycliffe's followers, John Hus, had been burned at the stake in 1415, with Wycliffe's Bibles used as kindling for the fire.

156. The title 'Saint' is conferred only by the Roman Catholic and Orthodox Churches

Saints play a big part in some denominations. The title is conferred by the Roman Catholic and Orthodox Churches after death through a process called canonisation, which is preceded by beatification. Saints are people not only judged to have lived a virtuous life, but to have performed (or been associated with) at least one verified miracle during their earthly lives.

Members of the Catholic and Orthodox churches believe that saints can intervene on behalf of people who are alive today, bringing health, healing, inner strength and prosperity. Most Protestants do not agree, but rather honour saints as inspirational figures, examples of holiness, dedication and self-sacrifice to be admired and emulated.

SACRAMENTS AND RITUALS

157. You could live as Yeshua taught and still not be regarded as a good Christian if you do not observe the sacraments

By the 11th and 12th Centuries, the Roman Church insisted that all stages of life from the cradle to the grave should be ruled by sacraments and marked by a church ceremony. The main Catholic sacraments are:

- Infant and/or adult baptism
- Confirmation
- Eucharist/communion
- Marriage
- Ordination
- Penance
- Last Rites

These seven are not all common to every denomination, but play an important part in Christian worship. Many churchgoers believe the sacraments were specified by Yeshua himself, and for most they are central to the Christian experience. Ironically in many churches you could live as Yeshua intended and still not be regarded as a good Christian if you do not attend services regularly and observe the sacraments.

158. There is no mention of infant baptism in the Bible

Infant baptism was not part of the Jewish tradition, so there is no mention of it in the Bible. Nor are there any references to Yeshua baptising anyone or urging anyone to be baptised in his lifetime. How, then, did the Christian practice of universal infant baptism come about?

As we have noted, the New Testament does not offer guidance on every aspect of living and infant baptism was one such 'gap'. Later, Bishop Augustine taught that children and adults who were not baptised would be condemned to hellfire after death.

Although there is no reference to *infant* baptism, the baptism of *adults* plays an important part in the New Testament. Yeshua himself was baptised by John the Baptist, which marked the start of his public ministry and set him on the path to arrest and crucifixion. Also, the Apostle Paul was in the habit of baptising converts, so by the time the gospels were written, it was probably a common practice, hence the passage at the end of the Second Gospel in which the Christ figure urges the disciples to 'go therefore and make disciples of all nations, baptising them in the name of the Father, and of the Son and of the Holy Spirit'.[232]

159. Confirmation dates back to the earliest years of Christianity

Confirmation started early in the history of Christianity. It reflects the Jewish practice of Bar Mitzvah in which a thirteen year-old boy is no longer considered a minor and takes responsibility for fulfilling the Torah's commandments.

Nowadays confirmation can be seen as the sealing of the covenant made on the infant's behalf by its parents in baptism. It takes place in most denominations when a child reaches adolescence, when he or she is considered able to think for themselves. Usually it is

---

[232] Matthew 28:19

preceded by a course of instruction and confers full membership of a local congregation on the recipient.

160. The Eucharist has produced irreconcilable disagreements between denominations

Eucharist is Greek for 'thanksgiving'. It's also known as Communion in Protestant churches and Mass in the Catholic Church, and is a powerful ritual for Christians. It commemorates the final meal that Yeshua took with his disciples, the 'Last Supper'.

The Last Supper is one of the rare episodes mentioned in both the gospels and the letters of Paul of Tarsus[233]. Paul's is the earliest known account (written around 54-55 CE) and is unusual since his letters otherwise show little interest in the details of Yeshua's life. Where else could he have got his information but directly from Cephas and Tiago, the disciples he met in Jerusalem?

Nowadays the image we have of the Last Supper is Leonardo Da Vinci's famous fresco, but the actuality could not have been like that. For a start, there was no table – diners lounged on the floor as was the tradition. According to the gospels, Yeshua shared bread and wine and asked his disciples to continue the practice in memory of him.

Although the Eucharist is recognised as a sign of unity amongst Christians, various traditions understand the Eucharist in different ways. The Catholic Church teaches that the priest has the power to change the bread and wine into the same substance as Yeshua's flesh and blood, but for most other denominations it is purely symbolic. As a result, the central idea of the Eucharist has given rise to often irreconcilable differences.

---

[233] 1 Corinthians 11:23-26

The bread and wine ritual remains a key part of Christian worship, but there are disagreements over whether Yeshua intended it to be repeated. But surely the answer is clear: Yeshua expected the Kingdom of G_d to arrive at any time. According to 'Mark' he said, 'Truly I tell you, I will never again drink of the fruit of the vine until that day when I drink it new in the Kingdom of G_d.'[234] In the Kingdom, the Eucharist would have been unnecessary.

161. In the gospels, Yeshua is very clear on adultery and divorce

The official line in most churches is that marriage is a lifelong commitment between a man and woman for the purposes of forming a family and rearing children. This has brought them into conflict with the law in countries where same-sex marriages have been legalised, but churches who revere the Bible have little choice but stick to their guns.

In the gospels, Yeshua says nothing about marriage but is very clear on sexual misconduct and divorce, and so is the Torah. It says bluntly, 'You shall not commit adultery.' [235] In the present day we see the terrible consequences for families, individuals and especially the young in ignoring this commandment.

For Yeshua, adultery was the only valid ground for divorce and the consequences extended beyond the immediate couple in that anyone who marries a divorced person could be guilty of adultery. 'Anyone who divorces their wife, except on the grounds of unchastity, causes her to commit adultery; and whosoever marries a divorced woman commits adultery.'[236] Although some

---

[234] Mark 14:25. The second and Third Gospels have similar quotes, but not the Fourth.

[235] Exodus 20:14

[236] Matthew 19:9

denominations take a more liberal line, the Catholic Church still only allows the dissolution of a marriage if declared null and void – that is, it never properly existed in the first place or was never consummated. Harsh perhaps to the modern way of thinking, but the gospels and Hebrew Scriptures are perfectly clear on this point.

162. Different denominations do not necessarily recognise each other's clergy

Ordination is the process by which individuals are appointed as clergy or bishops to perform the church's religious rites and ceremonies. The process varies by denomination. In most churches only an ordained person may administer the sacraments, namely conduct baptism, confirmations, marriages and funerals, hear confessions and lead the celebration of the Eucharist. This much is not in doubt - where they differ is in who exactly may be ordained. Many Protestant churches ordain women and some welcome homosexuals to the ministry, but only in 2014 did the Anglican Church vote to allow women bishops after years of deliberation. Previously traditionalists had blocked it by threatening to found a breakaway church and arguing that such a move would present an insuperable barrier to closer relations with the Catholic Church.

Statements made towards the end of 2013 by the new Pope Francis 1st were little short of revolutionary. His predecessors had held that the scriptures stated unequivocally that only men are suitable for the clergy since Yeshua chose only male disciples. Also, there are Biblical references, considered authentic, to women taking a subsidiary role in church[237], but Pope Francis said, 'In the future, let no door be closed to women that is open to men.'

---

[237]   E.g. 1 Corinthians 11:5, 1 Corinthians 14:33-35 and 1 Timothy 2:12

163. Confession of sins to a priest is provided for in many denominations

In the Catholic and Orthodox Churches, penance (confession of sins) is made through a priest. Absolution is then pronounced by the priest and received from G_d. Confession to a priest is also provided for in other denominations such as the Anglicans but not widely practised. On the other hand, some, such as the Lutherans and other 'non-conformist' churches, deny categorically that absolution can be obtained in this way.

The sacrament of Penance requires believers to examine their conscience, confess to a priest, express contrition and perform some act to repair the harm caused. The priest decides the act of reparation to be performed and grants absolution. The gravest sins must be confessed at least once a year followed by attending the Eucharist.

Priests are bound under the severest penalties to maintain absolute secrecy about sins revealed in confession. This occasionally brings them into conflict with the justice system since in most countries they are legally bound to report to the police if a serious crime has been committed.

164. The Sacrament of Anointing of the Sick is better known as the Last Rites

The Sacrament of Anointing of the Sick, formerly known as Last Rites or Extreme Unction, is a Catholic and Orthodox ritual intended to unite the sick person with Christ, give them strength and courage to endure their suffering, restore health (if conducive to the salvation of his or her soul) and prepare them to pass over to eternal life. It used to be administered mostly at the time of death, but nowadays is in much wider use. The practice also exists in some Protestant churches, but is not always considered a sacrament.

165. No one in Purgatory will go to hell

The word 'Purgatory' dates back to 12th Century Catholicism, but it is based on a much older tradition (among Jews, Buddhists and many other cultures) of purifying the dead and preparing the worthy to proceed to heaven. Only those who die in the state of grace but have not reached a sufficient level of holiness in life can be in Purgatory, and therefore no one in Purgatory will remain there forever or go to hell.

The notion of Purgatory as a geographical place only dates back to the Middle Ages; previously it was seen as a state of being of disincarnate souls. Yeshua makes no mention of it in the gospels. Presumably any such concept was unnecessary if the Kingdom of G_d was about to arrive.

166. The Book of Common Prayer was compiled by Thomas Cranmer in 1549

The Book of Common Prayer was the first English prayer book to include the complete forms of service for daily and Sunday worship. It contains the words for complete structured services and has remained the basis of Anglican worship and sacraments. Like the King James Bible, it's language is somewhat outdated but still held in high regard.

It was compiled by Thomas Cranmer (1489-1556) in the year 1549. Cranmer was Archbishop of Canterbury from 1533 - 1556 under King Henry 8th and briefly Edward 6th too. He was a leader of the English Reformation and responsible for establishing the basic structures of the Church of England after the split from Rome.

CHRISTIANITY TODAY

167. There are at least 38,000 different denominations

The first problem in ascertaining what Christianity teaches is to decide which form of Christianity since there are at least 38,000 different denominations.[238] The exact number is hard to determine; after all, what counts as a denomination? Most coexist harmoniously, but some are often at odds with each other.

There are three main groupings – Roman Catholic, Protestant and Eastern Orthodox (Russian, Greek, Syrian, Serbian etc.) Then there's a host of others, including Evangelicals, Seventh Day Adventists, Pentecostals, Christian Science, Coptic and Charismatics, and they're just for starters. In addition Spiritualists, Mormons, New Thought/Science of Mind/Christian Scientists, Moonies and many others quote Yeshua and draw inspiration from the Bible. Some of them also have their own versions of the Bible.

Where differences in doctrine exist, denominations try and respect each other's beliefs, but they don't always succeed. For example, Roman Catholic and Orthodox churches don't allow Protestants to attend their celebration of the Eucharist since they

---

[238] Source: ask.com. Other search engines give similar results.

do not agree over the status of the bread and wine used in the service. Moreover, many Christians don't buy into everything taught by their own church, for example, the Catholic Church's teachings on contraception. The Methodist Church bans alcohol, yet I knew a group of ministers who brewed their own beer and had regular get-togethers to sample the results.

Uniformity in Christian practice and belief has never existed. Even in its earliest days the Apostles Cephas and Paul were at loggerheads over whether non-Jews could be admitted. There are still major disagreements after nearly two thousand years, even though they all claim to worship the same G_d, follow the same Saviour and draw on the same scriptural sources.

168. The two genders 'sin in different ways'

Christianity is more contemptuous of sex than most other religions, but it doesn't stop the church devoting a great deal of attention to it. For example, in 2011 the Catholic Church published a study of confessions undertaken by a 95 year-old Jesuit scholar, Father Roberto Busa. He concluded that the two genders 'sin in different ways'. The most common sin for women was pride, while for men, the urge for food (gluttony) was only surpassed by the urge for sex.

On the very day I am writing this, a senior member of Northern Ireland's Free Presbyterian Church is on the radio supporting an edict to its members that they should not participate in line dancing – yes, line dancing - because this 'immoral practice' is an 'invitation to lust'!

169. Contraception 'harms true love and denies the sovereign role of God in the transmission of human life'

Prior to the 20th Century, contraception was generally condemned by all the major branches of Christianity. The church was opposed to contraception as far back as the time of Bishop Augustine. Some theologians regard it as murdering human beings even before their conception.

The Catholic Church teaches that all sex acts must be both unitive and procreative. It condemns the use of artificial birth control as intrinsically evil since it promotes 'immoral' behaviour, abstention being preferable. However, it recognises that sex cements the relationship between married (but not single-sex) couples and 'allows' them the right to engage in intercourse even when pregnancy is not a possible result, such as when one or both of the parties are infertile. Also, methods of natural family planning (such as the Rhythm Method) are morally permissible in some circumstances.

The Catholic Church's position on contraception has been reaffirmed many times in the last fifty years. For instance, the Vatican's Pontifical Council for the Family in 1997 stated that contraception 'harms true love and denies the sovereign role of God in the transmission of human life.' Condoms have come in for special criticism, even as a precaution against AIDS and other STDs. In 2003 the Vatican was accused by the BBC of intentionally spreading the lie that HIV can pass through the membrane of a condom, and in 2009, Pope Benedict asserted that handing out condoms is not the solution to combating AIDS and might even make the problem worse. He later softened his stance, claiming that the use of condoms can be a first step towards a more human way of living.

Most denominations do not regard contraception as inherently evil. Even the Catholic Church has not had its own way. Many Catholics have voiced their disagreement with the Church's stance on contraception, and many are known to use it. Catholics join non-Catholics in pointing out the role contraception can play in reducing global over-population, promoting women's rights, reducing the number of illegal abortions and preventing disease.

170. The tradition of celibate priests does not come from the Bible

In 1139, the Lateran Palace Council declared that all Catholic clergy must be unmarried and celibate. Since then they have been required disciplines and any priest who cannot conform ordered to leave the ministry. Prior to this they were not obligatory, although celibacy had come to be seen as an advanced state of holiness for monks, priests and bishops.

The thinking behind these requirements came from a rich tradition of regarding women and sexuality as distractions from spirituality. They also marked the clergy out from lay people, which was partly the aim. Nevertheless, many priests (and numerous popes) down the centuries have enjoyed the 'pleasures of the flesh', and not always with freely consenting adults as the church knows only too well to its shame!

The modern Catholic and Orthodox Churches continue to observe the tradition, but are not entirely united on a celibate priesthood. For instance, in 2013, a Cardinal called for the Church to end its insistence that priests be celibate, and urged the next Pope to allow them to marry. Celibacy left many priests struggling to cope with the demands of their ministry, he said; the burdens of being a priest were too much to bear alone without the support of a loving family. This was not the first time a senior Catholic had urged reform. Of course, most Christian denominations have no problems with married clergy being sexually active and married Anglican priests opposed to the ordination of women have been allowed to transfer to the Catholic Church and remain wed.

Perhaps the most interesting thing about his comments was his acknowledgement that the tradition of celibate priests did not come from the Bible nor was decreed by G_d. 'It is obviously not of divine origin,' said the Cardinal[239]. Indeed, neither the words 'celibate' nor 'celibacy' appear in the holy book. The gospels say Yeshua was strict on adultery and divorce, but they say nothing about celibacy. Indeed, coming from a culture in which family and children were highly valued, it is most unlikely that bachelorhood or abstention within marriage were seen as desirable.

171. There are no mentions of homosexuality in the gospels

Although there are no references to homosexuality or lesbianism in the gospels, there are several in the Hebrew Scriptures and the Apostle Paul roundly condemned homosexual practices. He warned against sexual misbehaviour of every kind, including sodomites and male prostitutes. He believed they went against the spirit of the new religion and excluded practitioners from the Kingdom of Heaven.

Anti-gay campaigners usually cite Yeshua's comments on adultery as covering homosexuality too, but whether he was advocating the kind of discrimination seen throughout Christian history, which continues to this day in some parts of the world, is a moot point. In October 2014 a measure backed by Pope Francis to make the church a more welcoming place for homosexuals was soundly defeated by a vote of Bishops. It remains to be seen whether this will be reversed in the coming years.

---

[239] There's a twist. A few hours after this Cardinal had made his plea, the news broke that he had been accused of 'inappropriate contact' with several (male) priests thirty years before. G-d sure works in mysterious ways!

172. One of the great contradictions in Christianity is how a loving G_d could create a world of such suffering

Until the late Middle Ages Christians were encouraged to welcome suffering as their Saviour supposedly welcomed his.[240] Martyrdom was highly prized and regarded as a sure road to sainthood. Some deliberately sought out suffering, believing that it would speed their progress to eternal life. Hundreds of thousands met their fate at a burning stake, on the gallows, a rack or quartering blade.

The question of how an all-powerful, loving G_d could create a world of such suffering, misery and disease is one of the great contradictions in Christianity. Theologians conclude that it is because humans have been granted free will. We make our own choices, but if we choose unwisely we must suffer the consequences. The doctrine of free will allows the faithful to explain away most of the tragedy and hardship in the world. G_d created the world and dictated the rules but allows humans in their ignorance to mess it up and suffer the consequences.

In the millennium or so during which the Hebrew Bible was written, natural disasters such as floods, drought and plague were interpreted as G_d's punishment for human failings. This attitude still persists today in some circles. For instance, in 2005 an Irish clergyman declared the recent Tsumani to be G_d's judgement on Asia for not being Christian, and a local councillor in the UK claimed in January 2014 that the reason Britain had recently been beset by storms and floods was because the government had acted 'arrogantly against the Gospel' by passing a law permitting same sex marriage. 'Is this just 'global warming' or is something more

---

[240] Two gospels dispute this by implication. The Third Gospel says he sweated blood as he awaited his fate and the Second that he cried out 'My G_d, my G_d, why have you forsaken me?' from the cross – hardly the words and actions of a man welcoming suffering.

serious at work here?' he asked. One wag commented that if flooding parts of the Thames Valley is the best G_d can do these days as opposed to raining fire and brimstone, we should be more worried about G_d's waning powers than the meteorological powers of gay people!

But how can giant storms, earthquakes and tsunamis, famines, droughts and plagues a matter of free will? Do people bring these on themselves by disobeying G_d's laws? If a family's house is flooded, a man's business goes bankrupt, a woman loses a baby prematurely or a young child dies in a road accident, is it because they have sinned? You, the reader, must decide, and if you decide that it is so, then it's true. For you.

173. Creationism originated in the 1920's

In some quarters (most prominently in the USA) Christianity has been hijacked by fundamentalists[241] who reject Darwin's Theory of Evolution in favour of the doctrine of Creationism. Evolutionists believe that all life evolved from tiny microbes in the sea. Those best suited to their environment thrived, multiplied and gradually became fish, amphibians, reptiles, birds, mammals, and finally us. Evolution is backed up by over one hundred and fifty years of rigorous scientific research.

Creationism only originated in the 1920's. Previously most Christians read the Adam and Eve stories as allegorical, which, of course, they are. Creationists believe that the stories in the first three chapters of Genesis are literally true; that G_d made the earth in six days culminating in humans, and Adam and Eve once roamed freely in the Garden of Eden. They insist that evolution cannot account for the diversity and complexity of life on Earth

---

[241] Yeshua was, of course, in his way a fundamentalist.

and the place of human beings within it. They cannot accept that humans could have evolved from apes.

Scientists are as convinced as they can be that evolution is no longer a wild theory, but a proven fact. It shows that the two Genesis creation stories are myths – as we've seen, they even contradict each other! Moreover, the process of creation is not yet finished. Human beings are still evolving.

However, there is a third explanation which is gaining favour - intelligent design. Unlike creationists, supporters don't dismiss evolution outright, but argue that there's more to it than organisms adapting to their environment and the survival of the fittest. They believe some organising intelligence is overseeing the process. Is this just another name for G_d? It depends what you mean by 'G_d' of course. I'll have more to say about this later.

174. Creationists assert the Earth is only 6,000 years old

Creationists (and many Muslims) believe that creation took place a mere six thousand years ago. They reject techniques which scientists use to date substances precisely (such as carbon dating) as inaccurate and invalid.

Why 6,000 years? In the 17th Century, the much admired scholar Irish Archbishop James Ussher (1581 – 1656) calculated that the world was created on the night preceding 23rd October 4004 BCE. He did this by working back from the birth date of Yeshua, assuming this to be December 25th in year zero, which we now know to be incorrect. He counted the generations listed in the biblical genealogies until he arrived back at Adam and Eve, then made assumptions about the number of years between each generation. It is on this spurious calculation that Creationists rely when asserting that the Earth is only 6,000 years old and that humans coexisted with the dinosaurs.

I asked a Creationist to justify this belief, bearing in mind that the scientific evidence indicates the Earth is around 4.5 billion years old[242]. He said that G_d makes it *appear* a lot older than it is. When I asked him why G_d would want to fool us in this way, he couldn't answer.

175. Yeshua taught that justice should be at the heart of government and social structures

In essence capitalism is just one way of organising the production and exchange of goods and services, but some Christian politicians and preachers believe it to be the natural order decreed by G_d and must be allowed to operate unrestrained. To other Christians, it is inherently evil, a legally-sanctioned means for the strong to make themselves rich at the expense of the weak, just as the wealthy religious and civil leaders of Yeshua's day exploited the poor.

Other than need, the driving forces of unfettered capitalism are, of course, greed, inequality and envy. In this respect nothing has changed since the gospel era. Yeshua had strong views on greed. 'Take care! Be on your guard against all kinds of greed, for one's life does not consist of the abundance of possessions.'[243] The Hebrew Scriptures warned against envy: 'You shall not covet your neighbour's house.... or anything that belongs to your

---

[242] Based on evidence from the radiometric age dating of meteorite material. 4.5 billion years is consistent with the ages of the oldest-known terrestrial and lunar samples.

[243] Luke 12:15

neighbour.' [244] Hence the early Christians practised communal ownership and no debt.

Modern Christians tend to emphasise the aspects of Yeshua's teachings that most serve their purposes. Some home in on his pronouncements on personal morality; others are more persuaded by his teachings on fairness and equality. But both are important. Yeshua taught that sharing and social justice are not just matters of individual conscience and behaviour, but should be at the heart of government, commerce and social structures – irrespective of the personal morality of the beneficiaries.

176. Christianity has always had an uneasy relationship with science

Philosophers have never had any problem incorporating spirituality into their world view, but scientists and theologians have often had an uneasy relationship. Some scientific discoveries have appeared to question the very basis of religion, and consequently some religions have resisted the scientific method.

The problem for Christians is that some of the statements in the Bible are just plain wrong by modern scientific standards. For example, at the time the Genesis creation stories were written, the Hebrews believed that the Earth at the centre of the universe, it was flat and covered by a dome above which were 'the waters'. Occasionally the dome leaked (it rained). The sun and stars were fixed to the inside of the dome, and below the ground was the place of the dead, portrayed by the ancient Greeks as Hades. It's hardly worth stating that we know better now.

---

[244] Ten Commandments, Exodus 20:17. To covet is to wish for longingly at someone else's expense.

In the Middle Ages, scientists such as Galileo Galilei (1564 – 1642) were harshly treated for publishing theories which were perceived to contradict Biblical teachings. Nicolaus Copernicus (1473 – 1543) published an astronomical model in 1543 which had the Sun at the centre of the Universe and the Earth and the other planets rotating around it. He did not attract the censure of the Catholic Church at the time, but Galileo was not so lucky a century later when he propounded a similar view. The church declared his findings false and contrary to scripture and forbade him to promote his theory.

Galileo later defended his views in '*Dialogue Concerning the Two Chief World Systems*', which alienated the Pope and the Jesuits, both of whom had supported him up until this point. He was tried by the Holy Office, found guilty of heresy and forced to recant. He spent the rest of his life under house arrest. It took 359 years to rectify this wrong. In 1992, Pope John Paul 2nd acknowledged in a speech that the Catholic Church had erred in condemning Galileo.

For several hundred years, science and religion staged an uneasy standoff. Scientists avoided making contentious statements about religion vice versa. Then came Charles Darwin, the author of 'The Origin of Species' and proponent of evolution. He was declared 'an enemy of God' for daring to advocate a theory that refuted the church's view of creation. Even so, he never lost his belief that G_d was the creative force responsible for blueprint for the universe. He wrote, 'When I wrote *The Origin of Species*, my faith in G_d was as strong as that of a bishop.'

Some pioneers of science had no difficulty seeing science and religion as compatible. Albert Einstein was viewed as a heretic by the church, yet he had a profound belief in G_d as a universal mind, spirit or creative intelligence that transcended the universe and was beyond our comprehension. He and many others, including Sir Isaac Newton and the 'Father of Quantum Mechanics', Max Planck, shared a sense of humility and awe at what they discovered in the natural world and gave the credit to this creative intelligence.

Nowadays the church is more comfortable with scientific research. The Catholic Church, for instance, employs ordained scientists to investigate such diverse subjects as the big bang, epigenetics and global warming, but their starting point is always the Bible teachings, not the observed data. In other words, they seek to fit the data to the Bible teachings, not find the best explanation that fits the data. We are without doubt gaining a greater understanding of *how* the material universe works, but are no nearer to understanding *why* the universe is as it is than were the ancient Greeks.

177. Reincarnation is mentioned in the gospels

Reincarnation forms part of the belief system of hundreds of millions of humans around the world, especially those in the Indian traditions. Most Buddhists and Hindus believe in it, so do spiritualists, as did Plato, St Francis of Assisi, Bishop Augustine, Goethe, Emerson and Pythagoras. It also plays an important part in the philosophy of Spiritualism and many African religions.

The philosopher and theologian Origen summed up his belief in reincarnation in two sentences. 'The soul has neither beginning nor end. (They) come into this world strengthened by the victories or weakened by the defeats of their previous lives.' Reincarnation was also a widespread belief among 1st Century Jews, and there is strong evidence that the early church embraced it until the

Council of Constantinople in 553 CE when it was officially declared anathema, at the instigation of the Emperor Justinian.

It's possible that most direct references to reincarnation were removed before the New Testament reached its final form, but they failed to get rid of them completely. For example:

- The Second Gospel hints that the disciples thought that Yeshua could be Elijah or Jeremiah reborn[245].
- The Fourth suggests the author thought it possible for a man's blindness to be due to his or his parents' sins in a previous life[246].
- In the First Gospel Herod Antipas also thought that Yeshua may be the reincarnation of John the Baptist - 'Mark' quotes Herod as saying, 'John, who I beheaded, has been raised.'[247]

Supporters of reincarnation use it to explain the amazing feats of childhood prodigies such as Mozart and some of the extraordinary 'déjà vu' incidents that people experience which, they argue, show that they really have been there before in a past life. Of course there's no proof that the soul of a deceased person can return in another body. Some claim that it's possible to remember our previous lives, but most of us can't, and perhaps that's a blessing. Isn't it better to concentrate on our present life?

Christianity teaches that we will one day face a Day of Judgement at which all our thoughts and actions will be considered and then G-d will decide whether to admit us to the Kingdom. But would a fair-minded loving G_d apply the same standards to everyone irrespective of where or when they were born and how talented

---

[245] Matthew 16: 13

[246] John 9:2

[247] Mark 6:16, Luke concurs (Luke 9:7-9)

or dim-witted they may be? Is it sensible to argue that a soul is created at a fixed point in time (conception) then survives the body and lives forever? How can there be a beginning but no end?

We don't know. We can't prove or disprove reincarnation, but we know that life is a continuing experience of growth in which we undergo challenges in order to raise our consciousness. If you choose to believe that the process continues over several lifetimes, then of course it's true. For you.

178. Gender equality has had a tough time in the Christian church

Gender inequality is hard-wired into the Hebrew tradition, the New Testament letters, church history and current practice in some denominations.

In Yeshua's day, the Purity Laws that ruled Jewish religious practice decreed that women were less pure than men due to their natural bodily processes of childbirth and menstruation. Women could not inherit property and were not legally recognised as valid witnesses. Moreover, women didn't count when determining descent. This is reflected in the writings of the Apostle Paul. Paul seemed to have a problem with women and has often been accused of misogyny; maybe his personal relationships with them were problematic. Paul was a celibate. He saw marriage as a concession to human (male) frailty but grudgingly conceded it was better to marry than burn with lust. He did not regard women as suitable leaders. He wrote that a husband in the head of his wife[248] and that women should not be permitted to speak in church.[249]

Paul's First Letter to Timothy gives advice for running a church. 'I permit no woman to teach or have authority over a man; she is to keep silent,'[250] it says before telling women that their salvation comes from having children provided they continue in faith

---

[248]   1 Corinthians 11:5
[249]   1 Corinthians 14:33–35
[250]   1 Timothy 2:12

and love and holiness. What do celibate nuns who devote their lives to the church make of that? But there are many reasons for not relying on these words. For a start, Paul didn't write them; the letters to Timothy were written thirty years after his death. Women played their full part in the early Christian movement, which brought condemnation from their Jewish neighbours. By the end of the 1st Century some Jewish Christians thought it had gone too far; perhaps 1 Timothy was part of their attempt to redress the balance.

Rome was a male-dominated society. When the Romans adopted the new religion, the authorities did not want to see women elevated because they were thought to be a distraction and carry a greater burden of sin than men. The story of Eve and the serpent in the Garden of Eden was seen as an allegory for their wickedness. This attitude was perpetuated through the Middle Ages. Typical is a Catholic guidebook published in 1486, the Malleus Maleficarum (literally the Witches Hammer), which was used to justify the widespread torture and murder of women. It instructed believers on how to spot witches and what to do with them, arguing that women were more credulous and therefore more susceptible to the influence of the devil. Also, because they were said to have slippery tongues, they shared the evil they knew, so they had to be rooted out and eliminated.

The Roman Catholic and Orthodox Churches still insist on a male only clergy because, they argue, Yeshua is said to have chosen only male disciples. In addition, they now have to defend 1600 years of tradition. We only have to go back a century and a half to find that all 'right thinking' people believed that educating women would be futile since their pretty heads would explode under the pressure of too much knowledge! But perhaps women's role is unjustly downplayed in the New Testament writings; for instance, Acts concentrates solely on the male disciples and says much less about the activities of Yeshua's women followers.

Nowadays Paul's comments on slavery and eschatology are rightly condemned as a feature of his times, but in some circles his views on women remain sacrosanct.

179. Women: Change is in the air

Statements made towards the end of 2013 by the new Pope Francis, on doctrine, women priests, homosexuals and respect for other faiths suggested that change is in the air. On women he said, 'In accordance with our new understanding, we will begin to ordain women as cardinals, bishops and priests. In the future, it is my hope that we will have a woman pope one day. Let no door be closed to women that is open to men.'

This is nothing short of revolutionary. The ordination of women in protestant churches has caused huge difficulties in relationships with the Roman Catholic and Eastern Churches, which have in any case never fully recognised protestant ordinations. They argued that the scriptures state unequivocally that only men are suitable for the clergy, since Yeshua chose only male disciples and there are authoritative Biblical references to women taking a subsidiary role in church.[251] Yet women clergy have proved their worth for many years, although the Anglican Church only allowed women to become bishops in 2014 following years of deliberation.

Aren't many of the feminine traits the essence of spirituality? Yeshua certainly thought so. The gospels say he cared deeply for women, and he frequently put his reputation on the line by

---

[251] Op cit

mixing with them, praising them and showing them respect. Even so, it would be unreasonable to expect Yeshua or the New Testament writers to lay down a blueprint for all time on a subject like male-female relations. Isn't it better to look at our world through 21st Century eyes, utilising 21st Century knowledge, than perpetuate the thinking and culture of 1st Century Palestine and 4th Century Rome?

TEN TEACHINGS FOR TODAY

180. Yeshua's teachings were primarily intended for his own people

First and foremost we must be aware that Yeshua's teachings were intended for his own people and specific to his time and place. His core message was that the Kingdom of G_d would come within a generation and redeem the Jewish nation, as promised in the Hebrew Scriptures. Like his mentor John the Baptist before him, this was his stated purpose, his reason for becoming a preacher, and why he chose the perilous path of confronting the religious authorities. It is debatable whether he looked much beyond the coming of the Kingdom which, after all, would sweep away the errors and inequities he was challenging.

The issues with which Yeshua and the early Christians were preoccupied – Jewish Law and Religious Practice, the Temple, the coming of the Kingdom and so on - for the most part seem incomprehensible to modern humans. Moreover our ever greater knowledge of the universe invalidates many of their 1st and 2nd Century understandings.

181. Yeshua never had the opportunity to verify the church's teachings

As we've observed, most of the church's teachings took shape long after Yeshua's death, so he never had the opportunity to verify them. But if he had, what would he have said? What would he have said to the bishops and theologians who formulated doctrine in the 4th and 5th Centuries? Would he have approved the Nicene Creed? Would he have recognised himself as one third of the Holy Trinity? Would he have agreed with Bishop Augustine's views on original sin? What would he make of the Christian sacraments? Would he have approved of the Book of Common Prayer and similar texts? How would he feel about the way he is portrayed now?

We don't know for sure, but we can make inferences based on the evidence available to us. We can look back on the 1st Century world with the benefit of hindsight and apply 21st Century scholarship. We can examine the ancient texts in a way that wasn't possible even a hundred years ago, drawing on new insights and sources that weren't available then. If it casts doubt on any of the basic tenets of the Christian religion, then so be it. As the Gershwins wrote – and I paraphrase - whatever you're liable to read in the Bible, it isn't necessarily so!

Our priority must be to address the spiritual and religious needs of the present. Yeshua was a man of his time, and all we can do is harmonise our spiritual quest with his. Some of his teachings have no relevance today; others still have enormous relevance because they teach us how to live better.

This isn't the place to give a full and detailed account of the gospel teachings, so I have picked out ten teachings attributed to Yeshua that I find insightful and have tried to apply in my life. They are consistent with the best guidance that practical psychology has to offer. I present them in alphabetical order, not order of importance.

182. Ask in prayer

The gospels say that Yeshua prayed frequently and encouraged his disciples to do the same. He taught them to go into their rooms, shut the door and pray to the Father in secret.[252] Christians are encouraged to pray in the same manner although in church prayers are offered collectively and are usually formal and ritualistic. Yeshua wanted everyone to find their own way to pray, not follow prescribed formats parrot-fashion.

Although the gospels give numerous instances in which Yeshua spent time in silent contemplation,[253] there is no record of Yeshua expressly teaching meditation even though it was part of the Hebrew tradition.[254] Meditation is not endorsed by every Christian denomination. I was once told by an evangelical Christian that meditation is a dangerous practice because it opens the mind up to the influence of the devil!

'Ask and it will be given to you; search and you will find; knock, and the door will be opened for you,' proclaimed Yeshua.[255] Unfortunately this has widely been taken out of context. Yeshua was not talking about earthly riches but spiritual ones – wisdom, perception, insight, knowledge and righteousness. From these all good things flow.

Modern studies, especially the work of Dr Larry Dossey,[256] medical practitioner and researcher, testify to the power of prayer,

---

[252]   Matthew 6:6

[253]   In contemplation one focuses on an idea and allows it to expand and acquire deeper meanings.

[254]   E.g. Psalm 46, 'Be still and know that I am God;' and Psalm 37, 'Be still before the Lord and wait patiently for him.'

[255]   Matthew 7:7-8 and Luke 11:9-10

[256]   E.g. *Healing Words: The Power of Prayer and the Practice of Medicine*, HarperOne, 2011

especially in the field of healing. I do not know how it works, but I know it does. Yeshua's advice to his disciples on prayer is as relevant today as ever it was.

183. Faith is the antidote to fear

There are two interpretations of the word 'faith':

1. Believing in something we've heard, read or been told, even if there's no proof and it seems implausible. This is how the word is normally used in church. The more you believe it, the stronger your 'faith' and the more admirable you are!
2. Trust in the process of life; that Spiritual Law works and is infallible, and accords with our experiences.

Yeshua's 'faith' was the latter. He taught that the Intelligence that created us also provides the means to sustain us. We should let go of worry and fear thoughts, get in tune with Spirit and let life express itself through us. 'Therefore I tell you, do not worry about your life.... Can any of you by worrying add a single hour to your span?' Nothing is impossible to those who have faith. 'All things can be done for the one who believes.'[257]

Sometimes we have to suspend disbelief and trust that if we sow the right seeds and nurture them, we will reap our harvest. Every word, every action has its consequences, and these consequences can rebound on us: 'In everything do to others as you would have them do to you; for this is the law....'[258] But it is not just words and actions – every thought, spoken or unspoken, has an effect. Good

---

[257] Mark 9:23
[258] Matthew 7:12

thoughts lead to good actions; bad thoughts cause inner conflict and impact on our speech and behaviour, thereby affecting others.

What is the main impediment to love and faith? Fear! What is the main impediment to fear? Love and faith!

184. Acid only harms the vessel that contains it

Oscar Wilde said, 'Always forgive your enemies. Nothing annoys then so much.' This is not the reason why Yeshua said we should forgive. When we forgive we heal our own pain and our bodies feel less tense. The person or event we've forgiven becomes a memory, no longer charged with negative emotion, whereas anger, bitterness and the lust for revenge cloud our judgment and stress us by flood the body with toxic chemicals and causing the muscles to tighten. It's said that acid only harms the vessel that contains it.

Forgiveness is not about condoning wrong doing or letting wrongdoers off the hook, but about taking responsibility for our lives. We forgive for ourselves, to get rid of the harmful 'stuff' we carry around with us. Indeed it usually makes no difference to the person(s) we forgive, and whether they deserve to be forgiven is not our concern.

Forgiveness opens the door to reconciliation - ending conflict and re-establishing cordial relations. Yeshua said if we are in dispute with someone, we should put everything else aside and first be reconciled to our adversary.[259] Seek peace within by letting go of negative thoughts. 'Whatever house you enter, first say, 'Peace to this house!'' Not only will you confer your peace on others, but also it will return to you.[260]

---

[259] Matthew 5:25
[260] Luke 10:5-6

When Yeshua was asked how many times we should forgive, he answered seven times seventy; [261] in other words, without limit. How do you know when you have really forgiven? When you no longer need to speak about the episode! And here's a point to ponder: Yeshua said that when you forgive, G_d will forgive you.[262] But does G_d need to forgive? To forgive someone you first have to blame them – does G_d blame? The Hebrew Scriptures and the gospels thought so. Do you?

185. All who humble themselves will be exalted

Yeshua told his audiences, 'The greatest among you will be your servant. All who exalt themselves will be humbled, and all who humble themselves will be exalted.'[263] Those who try to make themselves appear important will eventually be upstaged, so, for example, if you are invited to a banquet, select the lowest seat for yourself and wait to be moved higher if invited by your host.[264]

How does this relate to 21st Century life? We've all seen arrogant, self-centred, overbearing people get their own way, but at what cost? We've also seen many get their come-uppance.

186. Love your neighbour as yourself

Yeshua stood for love. When challenged to identify the greatest commandment of all, he quoted from the Hebrew Scriptures. 'You shall love the Lord your G_d with all your heart, and with all your soul, and with all your mind, and with all your

---

[261]   Matthew 18:21-22

[262]   Luke 6:37-38

[263]   Matthew 23:11. Incidentally, there is not much evidence of Yeshua's humility in the Fourth Gospel discourses, unlike the Synoptics.

[264]   Luke 14:7-14

strength,' and 'love your neighbour as yourself. There is no other commandment greater than these.' [265]

But what is love? A trick of the hormones? A mere emotion? A means of long-term needs fulfilment? Or something more? For Yeshua it transcended all of these. Perfect love is fearless, non-discriminatory, unconditional, completely unselfish, endlessly forgiving and forever. A tall order indeed. How many 'loves' do you know that meet these criteria?

The best definition of love in the Bible comes from Paul of Tarsus in his First Letter to the Corinthians.

> Love is patient and kind. It is never jealous. It does not boast, it is not proud; it is never rude or self-seeking; it is not easily angered, and keeps no record of wrongs. Love takes no pleasure in evil and delights in truth; it is always ready to excuse, to trust, to hope, to persevere. [266]

I can't think of a better definition and I'm sure this is what Yeshua had in mind.

187. Non-attachment: put aside material concerns and focus on higher things

In the gospels, Yeshua urges a shift of mental focus from the physical world to the spiritual ready for the coming of the Kingdom. This means letting go of attachments to wealth, family, status and material goods. The Fourth Gospel states: 'Those who love their life lose it, and those who hate their life in this world will keep

---

[265]   E.g. Deuteronomy 11:13 and Mark 12:30-31
[266]   1 Corinthians, 13, 4-7

it for eternal life.'[267] In other words, put aside worldly concerns and focus on higher things. This isn't too difficult if you believe that the world is about to be transformed and material things are about to become redundant, but is extremely demanding if you do not. A wealthy young man baulked when Yeshua told him to sell his possessions and give the money to the poor – this was just too much to ask.[268]

In the gospels Yeshua saved his most disparaging remarks for those who were attached to their possessions and pointed out that material things are transient. 'Do not store up for yourselves treasures on earth, where moth and rust consume... but store up for yourselves treasures in heaven.... For where your treasure is, there your heart will be also.'[269]

Most of the great spiritual teachers were exponents of the simple life. Does this mean we have to deprive ourselves to get in touch with our spirituality? No – Yeshua certainly didn't. But there is a balance to be achieved between meeting our material needs and pursuing spiritual goals. Our needs are really very simple. Once we have a steady supply of the essentials, extra belongings make very little difference to our happiness. Socrates, an advocate of the simple life, expressed this succinctly. He loved going to the market in Athens, and when asked about this, he replied, 'I love to go and see all the things I'm happy without.'

We don't have to believe in a mythical kingdom to benefit from an attitude of non-attachment. Many of the stresses of modern life are caused by attaching ourselves to money and 'stuff', glamour, vanity and prestige. Even though he was surrounded by people in poverty Yeshua knew there was a better way to live.

---

[267] John 12:25

[268] Matthew 19:21

[269] Matthew 6:19-21

188. Non judgement: the measure we give will be the measure we get

We make judgments all the time. We judge the speed and direction of other vehicles, how much pepper to add to our food and the temperature of our bathwater. We also make judgements about the best way to handle situations. These are helpful judgements, but there's also another type: labelling things right or wrong, good or bad, making unfavourable comparisons and criticising others.

Yeshua warns us not to judge for we will be judged by our own judgements, and 'the measure we give will be the measure we get.' If we are harsh in our judgements, others judge us harshly. 'Why do you see the speck in your neighbour's eye, but do not notice the log in your own eye? .... First take the log out of your own eye (i.e. put your own house in order before criticising anyone else).'[270] Who are we to judge anyway? Do we see the big picture?

When we live by faith, love and forgiveness we lose the desire to judge and no longer feel the need to blame.

189. Non-resistance: do not resist an evildoer

Non–resistance is one of Yeshua's most important and least understood gospel teachings, and the one in which he contradicts the Hebrew Scriptures most clearly. The Hebrew Bible is perfectly clear on matters of revenge and retaliation. As part of a long passage detailing the punishments that should be applied for a wide range of offences, it states: 'If any harm follows, then you shall give life for life, eye for eye, tooth for tooth, hands for hand, foot for foot, burn for burn, wound for wound, stripe for stripe[271].'

---

[270] Matthew 7:1-5
[271] Exodus 21:23-24

Yeshua completely overturned this. 'You have heard that it was said, an eye for an eye, and a tooth for a tooth. But I say to you, do not resist an evildoer. But if anyone strikes you on the right cheek, turn the other also.'[272] This does not mean we should literally allow an attacker to hit us twice, but ignore the evil deed so it no longer has any power over us and align our thoughts and actions with a positive outcome.

What about terrorists, murderers, rapists and so on? And what about the Nazis – were we right to stand up to them? If we didn't meet their violence with ours, wouldn't we be giving in to a bully?' Not according to Yeshua. He said, 'All who take the sword will perish by the sword.' As Gandhi, Mandela and Martin Luther King showed, practising non-violent non-resistance withdraws spiritual energy from evil-doers, and anything starved of spiritual energy eventually loses its power. It worked in the case of the Soviet Empire in the 1980s and the ending of apartheid in South Africa.

If someone insults us or causes us harm, we should not try to get even but forgive them and mentally send a blessing. The alternative is tit for tat retribution. If the principle of non-resistance were universally applied all conflict would end, including inner conflict, but it's not easy. We risk ridicule and harassment when we refuse to retaliate; people call us 'weak' and 'a pushover'. 'Matthew's' Yeshua said, 'Blessed are those who are persecuted for righteousness' sake.'[273] That's one way we know we're on the right path.

---

[272] Matthew 5:39
[273] Matthew 5:10

190. Service: make selflessness the norm

According to the Third Gospel, John the Baptist said, 'Whoever has two coats must share with anyone who has none; and whoever has food must do likewise.' [274] This was a constant theme of Yeshua's ministry.

Modern life in the West is characterised by extreme selfishness, sanctioned by an economic system that encourages people to grab what they can before someone else does. Indeed, free market economists argue that unfettered greed is in the public interest, but just look at the facts. Over one thousand million people today live in a permanent state of starvation. A quarter of the world's population is denied the basic requirements of a decent life – good food, clean water, shelter, sanitation and health care. Another quarter have only a rudimentary education and no chance of well-paid and fulfilling work. In every country, including the most affluent, there are people living in absolute destitution. In these respects little has changed since Yeshua's day.

If life is to become the heaven we seek for all, selflessness must become the norm. We must look for opportunities to help others, give generously and receive graciously, knowing that giving with no thought of return enriches ourselves.

191. Wholeness

The Second Gospel says that the purpose of life is to become 'perfect, as your heavenly Father is perfect.'[275] This is our goal. A better translation may be 'complete' or 'whole', physically, mentally, emotionally and spiritually. A tall order indeed! We

---

[274] Luke 3:11
[275] Matthew 5:48

201 Things about Christianity You Probably Don't Know (But Ought To)

should strive for wholeness through love, faith and wisdom, rising above material consciousness and bringing out the perfection in our being. This is a lifelong quest which takes learning, effort, courage and determination. It's probably beyond most of us, but that's not the point. Going for it brings rewards; what matters is not arriving at the destination but enjoying the journey.

THE NATURE OF BELIEF

192. The world is run by a family of giant lizards

As a child, I was taught to respect other's beliefs, but only up to a point. I was to respect other people's tastes, political opinions and allegiances, but my Methodist parents also warned me to be suspicious of the Catholic family living next door, the Spiritualists across the road, men with long hair and anyone wearing a turban!

Respect for other's beliefs is a thorny one. Are we supposed to respect people who blow themselves up in crowded places taking dozens of innocent bystanders with them, or those who behead blameless people in the Syrian desert believing that they'll be venerated as martyrs in the next life?

A few year ago author David Icke achieved notoriety for claiming – in all seriousness - that the world is run by a family of giant lizards who disguise themselves as humans, including both George Bushes, the Queen of England, Tony Blair and many leading industrialists. Mr Icke, who has sold shiploads of books around the world, vehemently defends this position. How much respect should we accord to this belief?

Similarly, there are people all over the world who believe that a man came back to life two thousand years ago after dying on a cross and was last seen floating skyward on a cloud will one day return to Earth and rescue us from our misery and sin. We consigned Odin, Jupiter, Zeus and Thor to mythology years ago – yet Elohim, YHWH, Jehovah, Abba – whatever you want to call it – is still venerated.

Religion and superstition are essentially the same. They are both types of belief. The only difference is that religion is taken seriously and has much higher status. People readily apply logic to most areas of their lives, but religion is not subjected to the same standards of proof as, say, science, mathematics and psychology.

193. All religions are matters of belief

The existence or nonexistence of G_d is a belief. It can't be *proved* either way.

A belief is an idea or set of ideas that we accept as true. Beliefs are what we rely on when our knowledge is exhausted. People believe all sorts of things that don't have a shred of evidence to support them. Besides my beliefs are not the same as yours so we can't both be right about everything. Yet millions have died for their beliefs and continue to do so without troubling themselves with the facts!

Some beliefs are different in nature. If I believe that I will plummet to earth if I jump off a tall building and you believe that I won't, I am right and you are wrong. How do I know? Because the effects of gravity are observable, measurable, repeatable and consistent. Religious beliefs are not like this. They concern things that we do not know and can never know for sure. If we *knew*, they would cease to be *beliefs* and become *knowings*.

Beliefs can change, and they do when better ideas come along. In physics, Newton's model of the world has been superseded by Quantum Mechanics – but how do we know this isn't wrong too? How do we know that every belief we have won't turn out to be wrong one day? If I still believed what I was taught as a child, I would continue to believe that Adam and Eve were the first man and woman on earth, that Noah managed to squeeze two of every known animal onto a boat without them killing each other, Jonah spent three days in the belly of a whale and there's a big man in the sky who watches over my every move, listens in to my every thought, and will one day condemn me for eternity if I don't measure up. But I don't; the evidence is just too strong.

The mainstream churches have a long history of suppressing facts that conflict with their beliefs. It's not that the theologians involved were deliberately deceitful although some may have been, but because they were so immersed in their own notions of 'truth'. They dismissed inconvenient facts out of hand, but we shouldn't be too critical – isn't that what we all do every day?

194. Our beliefs create our experience of life

Our beliefs rule our lives and help to create our experience of life. They sit in our unconscious and influence us whether we are paying attention to them or not. And it doesn't matter if they are true, the effect is the same. An untrue belief is just as powerful as a true belief. We see the world not as it is, but filtered through our beliefs.

We humans can convince ourselves of anything if we really want to, and when we do our minds close and beliefs run the risk of turning into prejudices. We become so convinced that we are right that we seek and find 'evidence' to support our views even if we are wrong. We seek out people who agree with us and switch off to people who do not.

The Placebo Effect demonstrates how powerful beliefs can be. So does the Nocebo Effect, where inert substances cause harm simply because the recipient believes they can. Karl Marx famously referred to religion as the 'opium of the masses.' Perhaps 'placebo' or 'nocebo of the masses' would have been more appropriate.

195. Perhaps G_d is an information field

Before Einstein, the world was thought to be a collection of atoms and molecules behaving according to certain inviolable 'laws'. Space was exactly that – empty space, nothing there. Now we know that matter is merely energy condensed to a slow vibration and even space is not really empty: it is a presence, an inexhaustible potential that manifests in places as matter. What appears to us to be solid matter is actually 99.9999% empty space: billions of tiny particles flying in formation, all held together by an invisible force field. Incredibly, when subatomic particles are studied in detail, they do not actually exist. They are not particles like, say, particles of dust. Rather, they appear and disappear millions of times a second and move at inestimable speeds. Moreover, physicists state that we cannot assume they continue to exist when they are not being observed.

Everything, including us, came out of a formless world of energy. Somewhere in that field of energy is something that determines what we are and what we will become - information. Information is everywhere. It's in every wave and every particle; every atom and every cell. There's information we see (printed information, TV, internet, GPS) and information we don't see. Wherever we are, we are surrounded by and infused with information. We may not always have the means to access it but it's still there, just as a person without their mobile phone on cannot access a signal.

This is hardly a new idea. Thousands of years ago the Indian Rishis knew that matter is not ultimate reality and in his 'Theory of Forms' 2,500 years ago, Plato argued that behind every physical thing is the *idea* of that thing (i.e. information), and it is the idea that is real. The New Testament Letter to the Hebrews states that all visible things come from the invisible and are dependent on the unseen for their existence. More recently Max Planck (1858 – 1947), the theoretical physicist who originated quantum theory and won a Nobel Prize for his work on the atom in 1918, wrote:

> 'All matter originates and exists only by virtue of a force… We must assume behind this force the existence of a conscious and intelligent Mind. This Mind is the matrix of all matter.'

What exactly is this conscious and intelligent force, this stream of life? Frankly, I don't know, and nor do I believe anyone who says they know for sure. As Max Planck wrote, 'Science cannot solve the ultimate mystery of nature. And that is because, in the last analysis, we ourselves are a part of the mystery that we are trying to solve.'

In his book *Life After Death: The Burden of Proof,* Dr Deepak Chopra, one of the great modern spiritual thinkers, makes this statement:[276]

'Right now you are a bundle of information in mind and body. You have unique memories; your cells have undergone chemical changes shared by no one else in the world. When you die, none of this information will vanish, because it can't. There is nowhere for plus and minus, positive and negative to go since the field contains nothing but information. Therefore their only alternative is to recombine.'

---

[276] Deepak Chopra, *Life After Death: The Burden of Proof.* In the section, 'Thinking Outside the Brain.'

We are getting closer to solving the mystery; the only question is just how close will we get. Every generation, scientific knowledge advances and spiritual awareness unfolds. But what if G_d were an information field, *the ultimate* information field that provides the blueprint for the universe and everything in it? That constantly communicates with us and responds to our communication, reflecting our thoughts and words? Now *there's* an idea!

THE FUTURE

196. To be a Christian is to see the 21st Century world through 1st Century eyes

To be a Christian today is to see the world the same way as a small group of religious mavericks living in a tiny part of the world region nearly two thousand years ago. Why adopt their point of view? Why look at the 21st Century world through 1st Century eyes? Isn't it better to look at the 21st Century world through 21st Century eyes, drawing on 21st Century knowledge!

Wise spiritual seekers understand this. They do not dismiss the Christian tradition outright, but know that the scriptures must be read allegorically and metaphysically to access their real meaning. They acknowledge tradition but do not follow it blindly. You'll find many of them listed as authors in the glossary at the end of this book.

197. Yeshua bar Yehosef died a failure

How did Yeshua feel as he drew his last breath, knowing that his mission on earth had ended in failure? He promised that the world would be transformed within a generation, and it wasn't. It's a contradiction that has bedevilled Christianity for nearly two thousand years and continues to do so despite being repeatedly swept under the carpet by Christian apologists. The Church still teaches that he will return one day and the world will be transformed. They don't say when, which is probably just as well. But Yeshua was clear – *within the lifetime of his disciples*. It didn't happen.

Dr Diarmaid MacCullogh paraphrases Dr Albert Schweitzer in concluding that Yeshua's public ministry was built on a mistake:

- He believed the end of the world was coming – and soon
- He offered up his life to bring it on quicker
- The world did not end and G_d did not appear.
- He died a figure of failure and tragedy.[277]

The resurrection and ascension narratives allowed his followers to snatch victory from the jaws of defeat – and we've seen how questionable these are. Even then, it took an emperor's vision of a cross of light in the sky and the might of Rome to rescue the much maligned religion from obscurity and give it a future.

198. Truth is Truth for everyone for all time

To be a spiritual Truth, it must be true for everyone, everywhere and for all time. It stand to reason, doesn't it? There are other sorts of 'truth' of course, that vary from person to person. We speak of 'my truth' and 'your truth', inferring that something can be true for me but not you and vice versa. And it can.

But spiritual Truths cannot be like this. They must apply equally whether we live in Europe, the American Bible Belt, the Arabian

[277] Diarmaid MacCulloch, A History of Christianity, Penguin, 2010, page 860

Desert, the salt lakes of Utah, Tibet, the Andes or the Himalayas; in the 1st, 4th, 10th or 21st Centuries CE; for men, women and children of all languages, races, abilities and ages; for those alive today, those who have passed on and those yet to be born.

Religions seldom satisfy these criteria. Most arose to meet the needs of a particular people at a particular place and point in history. Some are even restricted to a specific race, culture or genealogy.

Imagine if all the great religious teachers - Yeshua, Mohammed, the Buddha, Lao Tsu, the writers of the Bhagavad Gita, Mahatma Gandhi, Martin Luther King, Francis of Assisi and so on sat round a table together. They would 90% agree. Yet we squabble over the differences (the 10%) and even go to war over them.

There is only one Truth (with a capital 'T'): let's seek it together and concentrate on what unites – not divides – us.

199. Christianity is not about good deeds but blind faith

Does Christianity help or hinder us realising our spirituality? What is spirituality anyway?

Spirituality is a deep appreciation of our non-physical essence coupled with a process of personal growth and transformation. In contrast, religion is a formalised set of beliefs and rituals presented within a recognisable organisational structure. It's an uncomfortable fact for those who like formality and ceremonials in religion that the Yeshua was not a huge fan of them.

Not long ago, a prominent former UK government minister presented a TV programme on the future of Christianity. She had resigned from the Church of England when they voted to allow women clergy and became a Roman Catholic, arguing that women are not equipped to become priests. Since retiring from politics she has contributed to many discussion shows. During the programme, she debated with a Humanist. He argued, as a Humanist would, that the whole basis of Christianity is flawed. There are no gods, no angels, no devil and no miracles, and morality doesn't depend on believing in these things.

'Don't you believe in love and forgiveness, and being kind to each other?' she countered. He said of course he did, but that didn't make him a Christian; all the great religions teach love, compassion, peaceful conduct and right living. Humanism does too. They're largely common sense and do not need Christian theology to support them. And he's right. *Because it's not these things that define Christianity.* There's a lot more to it than loving your neighbour and treating others as you would like to be treated.

Even following the gospel teachings of Yeshua is not enough. *It's not even the point.* Far more important for Christians is to believe certain things about him – who he was, why he came to Earth, his place in the Holy Trinity and what became of him after he died. The religion's greatest apostle, Paul of Tarsus made this very clear: if we have absolute faith in Yeshua's death and resurrection, we redeem ourselves and take our place in the Kingdom of G_d. *This, not one's good deeds, is what distinguishes a Christian from a non-Christian.*

200. Christianity offers hope, comfort and membership of a community

It is my contention that Christianity in its traditional, literal form cannot survive in the long term because its basic tenets continue to be based on 1st Century understandings of the world and much of its language is steeped in the symbolism and imagery of the Middle Ages. It's time to apply 21st Century thinking. It is in terminal decline. It must change or it will surely die.

How will it change? Well, slowly. People don't readily change their minds. As Einstein observed, conventional wisdom changes because the people who hold the old ideas die off and are replaced by the next generation with new ideas. Outdated ideas are weakened with each successive generation until they disappear. Take slavery for example, a practice idea endorsed in the New Testament. Today hardly anyone would support it, yet only two hundred years ago it was widely thought to be the natural order of things. Racism, sexism, ageism and many other outmoded 'isms' have gone the same way.

What, then, does Christianity offer in the modern age? Irrespective of the flaws in the New Testament writings, many gain hope and comfort from its teachings. They benefit from membership of a community based on Christian principles. They value its heritage, continuity and the sense of security it brings. It also provides:

- A moral code that most of us can subscribe to and live by.
- A cultural framework.
- A vehicle for acknowledging and celebrating major life events (birth, adulthood, marriage, illness and death).
- The opportunity to give and receive charity.
- Some great teachings, such as love, compassion, non-resistance, non-judgement and forgiveness.
- A means to access our inner spirituality, through prayer, silence and contemplation.
- Support and solace in testing times.
- A social life centred on a church.

201. Christianity can hinder our spiritual progress

Given that spirituality is a deep understanding of our non-physical essence and its implication, that there is nothing standing between us and our Spiritual Selves and that our spirituality connects us to all things through the Great Information Field we call G_d, how helpful is Christianity in furthering our spiritual progress?

In his best-selling book, *Further Along the Road Less Travelled*, M. Scott Peck pointed out that we are not all at the same place in terms of our spiritual growth and listed four stages on the spiritual journey. He acknowledged that people do not always fall neatly into categories and that there is always some overlap.

1. Stage One people have little or no interest in spirituality. They appear to have few moral principles, live chaotic lives and are frequently found in prisons or on the street. Some, however, rise to positions of power. Some Stage One people become aware that there's more to life than they're experiencing and convert to Stage Two. When this happens, it can be sudden, such as a dramatic conversion to 'born again' Christianity or something extreme such as Jehovah's Witnesses etc.

2. Stage Two people look to authority and are dependent on an organisation for their governance. This could be the military, a business, public institution or religious body. According to Peck, the majority of religious believers fall into this category, and certainly most Christians in the pews do. They rely on its teachings and rituals for stability and to deliver them from uncertainty. Stage Two people who outgrow the need for prescribed structures and rituals move towards Stage Three.

3. Stage Three people feel no need to look to an organisation for direction. They may not be religious in the usual

sense of the word, but value their spirituality and are often involved causes working for peace and justice. Stage Three people often regard Stage Two people as gullible, while Stage Two people feel threatened by them because of their lack of respect for conventional beliefs. As they develop, they begin to glimpse a bigger picture and may even begin to take an interest in some of the mythology that attracts their Stage Two neighbours. They begin to embrace Stage Four.

4. Stage Four individuals believe in the underlying connectedness between things. They are comfortable with the mystery of life and seek to explore it more deeply. They are inspired by the great religions, but not bound to them. At first sight, Stage Two and Stage Four people appear opposites, yet they have much in common. They know the same passages of scripture, but interpret them differently. Stage Three people are baffled by Stage Four. On the one hand, they aspire to their awareness and spirituality, while being puzzled about their interest in those old myths and legends.

Christianity is a Stage Two religion because it holds to the belief that it is the only true religion and all others are false. It has no truck with those Stage Three and Four people who believe that there are many paths to higher consciousness. This is not just a Christian belief, of course – Islam, in particular, takes a similar view of itself. But if only Christianity is true, then Islam, Hinduism, Judaism, Buddhism and the rest are untrue; and if any of the others are true, then Christianity must be false.

If I have to believe in a virgin birth, voices from the sky, walking on water, dead and decomposing bodies coming back to life and a man being carried up to heaven on a cloud before I can realise my spirituality, then Christianity hinders me. It's a barrier. I can study it, learn from it and borrow the sayings and parables that make sense to me. The rest I can reject without fear of eternal damnation (a loving G_d wouldn't do that to me anyway). That's what more and more people are doing in this enlightened age; long may it continue.

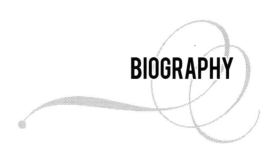

BIOGRAPHY

David Lawrence Preston is a teacher, life coach, trainer and author and a leading authority in the area of life enrichment and spiritual development based in the UK. He helps people to transform their lives through his books, talks and workshops. He is the author of *365 Steps to Self Confidence, 365 Ways to be your own Life Coach and 365 Steps to Practical Spirituality* and had appeared many times on UK radio and TV.

He first became interested in these subjects after a life-changing experience in Moscow and has since taken his knowledge and insights to five continents. He has worked with countless individuals and organisations, where his warmth, humour and sincerity are well received by audiences.

David was brought up a traditional Christian, but his quest for truth and inclusivity led him to explore a wide range of religious and spiritual ideas. As he wrote in *365 Steps to Practical Spirituality,* what unites the major religions is far greater than what divides them Ninety percent of their teachings are the same, yet even today wars are being fought over the other ten percent. David teaches that no one religion has exclusive rights to the truth and many different paths are open to us.

His website is www.davidlawrencepreston.co.uk and his blog, which covers a wide range of topical subjects, can be accessed at http://blog.davidlawrencepreston.co.uk/. He also manages a site dedicated to health and wellbeing, www.feelinggoodallthetime.com. You can also find him on Twitter, @DavidPres, @Feelinggoodatt and Facebook.

ACKNOWLEDGEMENT

I writing this book I owe a great debt to some of the great scholars and writers of the last century and a half who have shone a light into the past and laid bare the origins of the Christian religion. Here I include Drs Marcus Borg, Bart Erdman, Geza Vermes, Diarmaid MacCullogh, Paula Fredriksen and others who first dissect the Christian myth and then meticulously remove the flesh from the bones. Paula Fredriksen's book, 'From Jesus to Christ' inspired me so deeply that as soon as I put it down I immediately read and re-read the New Testament several times.

However, all too often, after presenting loads of evidence that mainstream Christianity is built on shaky foundations, some of these become apologists for the very religion they discredit with their analysis! For example, Dr Robert Beckwith, who presented the C4 TV programme 'Who Wrote the Bible', showed that the Bible is anything but the word of G_d, yet still professed to be inspired and comforted by Christian ideas. That's like cutting off the legs of a chair you're sitting on.

Similarly Professor Marcus Borg is a leading authority on Christianity and the Bible whose books should be better known, but after demolishing the Christian myth with his scholarship admits to getting inspiration and succour from the Anglican faith.

Bishop John Shelby Spong wrote a devastating attack on the religion[278], giving countless examples of biblical ideas that are shaped by a redundant world view, then pledged his allegiance to it. He recognises this himself when he writes, tellingly, 'I suspect that the next generation might even dismiss me as an old-fashioned religious man who could not quite cut the umbilicus to the past in order to enter the future.' Well, I have the greatest respect for his scholarship and his courage but yes, you're right Bishop!

I also greatly admire the scholarship of Dr Geza Vermes and others who have the temerity to point of out that Yeshua bar Yehosef, the carpenter from Nazareth, was actually born, lived and died a Jew!

Diarmaid MacCulloch author of the thousand page History of Christianity doesn't attempt to criticise Christian beliefs, merely report their history. Then, despite laying bare its flaws and the cruelties performed in its name, he calls himself 'a candid friend of Christianity'. Some friend! On page eleven he writes, 'I live with the puzzle of wondering how something so apparently crazy can be so captivating to millions of other members of my species.'

I was inspired in 2001 by Jeremy Bowen's brilliant BBC series, Son of God, which drew on archaeological evidence to reveal the history and geography of the Biblical lands in the 1st Century. A version is available on YouTube.

I have greatly enjoyed reading CJ Werleman's commentaries on the Bible, although Mr Werleman's aggressive attitude and crude language can easily offend.

---

[278] In 'Why Christianity Must Change or Die.'

I also owe a great debt to the great religious thinkers of the past couple of centuries who risked censure when pointing out the nonsense perpetrated in the name of the church and the hypocrisy of many of the church authorities of their day. Here I include Dr Albert Schweitzer, Phineas Parkhurst Quimby, Charles Fillmore and Dr Eric Butterworth.

And finally to Rev Tom Thorpe, an inspiring teacher with an encyclopaedic knowledge of the Bible from whose instruction I have learned immensely.

RECOMMENDED READING AND VIEWING

Karen Armstrong, *St. Paul's Impact on Christianity*, Macmillan, 1983, ISBN-13: 978-0330281614.

Dr Robert Beckford, *Who Wrote the Bible*, Channel 4 TV, 2004, (DVD). Available on You Tube in some countries.

Professor Marcus Borg (1), *Meeting Jesus Again for the First Time: the Historical Jesus and the Heart of Contemporary Faith*, HarperSanFrancisco, 1995, ISBN 0-06-060917-6

Professor Marcus Borg (2), *Reading the Bible Again for the First Time: Taking the Bible Seriously but not Literally*, HarperSanFrancisco, 2001, ISBN 0-06-060919-2.

Professor Marcus Borg (3), *Speaking Christian,* HarperCollins, 2011, ISBN 978-0-281-06508-0. Not only identifies mistranslations of important Christian words, but explains what these words would have meant to the original authors in context.

Professor Marcus Borg (4), *Jesus: Discovering the Life, Teachngs and Relevance of a Religious Revolutionary,* HarperOne, 2006, ISBN 978-0-06-143434-1

Eric Butterworth, *Discover the Power Within You,* HarperSanFrancisco, 1992, ISBN 0-06-250115-1.

Kenneth C. Davis, *Don't Know Much About the Bible*, Perennial, 2004, ISBN 0-380-72839-7

Prof Bart D. Ehrman *Forged: Writing in the Name of God,* HarperOne, 201, ISBN-13 – 9780062012623. (Everything he has written is well researched and informative and borne out of personal experience.)

Prof Bart D. Ehrman) *How Jesus Became God*, HarperCollins, 2014, ISBN 978-0061778186.

Prof Bart D. Ehrman *God's Problem – How the Bible Fails to Answer Our Most Important Question – Why We Suffer,* HarperCollins, 2008, ISBN 978-0-06-157833-5

Paula Fredriksen, *From Jesus to Christ*, Yale University Press; 2nd Rev. Edition, 2000, **ISBN-13:** 978-0300084573

Timothy Freke and Peter Gandy, *The Jesus Mysteries – Was the Original Jesus a Pagan God?* Thorsons, 2000, ISBN-13: 978-0722536773

Father Joseph Girzone, *Joshua – A Parable for Today,* Prentice Hall, 1987, ISBN-13: 978-0684813462

Diarmaid MacCulloch, *A History of Christianity*, Penguin, 2010, ISBN 978-0-141-02189-8

Ken Palmer, Harmony of the Gospels, www.LifeofChrist.com 2, ©1999 Ken Palmer.

M. Scott Peck, *Further Along the Road Less Travelled,*

E. P. Sanders, *The Historical Figure of Jesus,* Penguin, 1993, ISBN 978-0-14-192822-7. (Authoritative attempt to piece together the evidence of Yeshua's human existence.)

E. P. Sanders, *Paul – A Very Short Introduction,* Oxford University Press, 1991, ISBN 978-0 -19-285451-3. (An excellent introduction to the life and teachings of Yeshua's leading apostle.)

Dr Albert Schweitzer, *The Quest of the Historical Jesus,* Dover, 2005, ISBN 13-978-0-486-44027-9 (A detailed account of scholarship into the historical Yeshua written in the late 19th Century.)

Bishop John Shelby Spong, *Why Christianity Must Change or Die,* Harper One, 1998, ISBN 978-0-06-067536-3 (Should be compulsory reading for all Christians.)

Rico Tice and Barry Cooper, *Christianity Explored,* The Good Book Company, 2002, ISBN 978-1-90488-934-2 (Conventional Christianity explained by wool-over-the-eyes believers.)

Prof Gerd Theissen, *The Shadow of the Galilean,* SCM Press, 1987, ISBN 978-0-334-02852-9 (An entertaining and insightful novel which reflects on the impact made by Yeshua in Palestine in his own time.)

Prof Geza Vermes, *The Changing Face of Jesus,* Penguin, 2000, ISBN 0-14-026524-4. (A scholarly book that examines the changing portrayal of Jesus in the Official Gospels, from the Palestinian Holy Man who inspired 'Mark' to the divine figure invented by 'John'.)

CJ Werleman, *God Hates You, Hate Him Back (Making Sense of the Bible),* Dangerous Little Books. 2009. (A stimulating review of the Hebrew Scriptures, but not for the faint-hearted.)

CJ Werleman, *Jesus Lied - He Was Only Human: Debunking The New Testament*, Dangerous Little Books, 2010, ISBN 978-0956427618. (Another stimulating read, but somewhat disrespectful.)

A. N. Wilson, *Jesus: His Life,* W W Norton & Co, 1992, ISBN 0-393-03087-3. (A critical look at the gospel stories and the archaeological evidence to construct a picture of the life and times of Yeshua bar Yehosef.)

Linda Woodhead, *Christianity – A Very Short Introduction,* Oxford University Press, 2004, ISBN 978-0-19-280322-1 (A balanced introduction.)

Printed in the United States
By Bookmasters